Out of Nowhere

A Personal Encounter with Life's Fickle Lottery

By Esther M. R. Hougham

Cover Design: Laura Masterson

Photograph of Butterfly on Front Cover
by Esther M. R. Hougham

ISBN-13: 978-1466257504

ISBN-10: 1466257504

This book is dedicated to all the brave bone marrow
transplant patients present and past, their loved ones,
the donors and the dedicated medical personnel of
Ward 3Z at McMaster University Hospital who make
it all happen so that some of us can have a chance at life.
Bob and Pat...I love you...thank you.

All profits from the sale of this book will be donated to
"The Bone Marrow Transplant Leukemia Research Fund"
at McMaster University Hospital.

PROLOGUE

At the age of 48, I was blindsided by life despite my efforts of eating right, exercising and being about as disciplined as anyone could be. Out of nowhere, I was diagnosed with a rare, terminal illness that affects one in a million individuals annually. Equally as rare, I survived against all odds. The lottery of life chose me as both its loser and winner. Here is my story.

Chapter 1

August 27th to August 31st

Six years have passed since "it" happened. I've waited this long to write my story because I was afraid that somehow I would jinx my good health by telling the tale.

It was a Saturday morning and that evening my husband, Bob, and his friend Mike were returning home from their annual Alaska fishing trip. I still had quite a few chores left to do prior to Bob's homecoming…the biggest job involved the trimming of about 25 ornamental shrubs. In my usual 100 mph speed, I trimmed the bushes, jumped in the shower and got myself ready to head to the hairdresser's for a color and cut at 10:30 a.m. I gave our two dogs, Dudley and Max, a pat and a cookie and told them I would be home soon.

As I stepped into the garage, the hot, stifling air reminded me of the record setting heat we had to endure that summer. Bob and I owned a farm; we rode and trained horses daily which was usually a fun job; however, because of the temperatures, I had found it unusually tiring and draining. I was looking forward to some cooler weather and hopefully feeling more energetic.

I arrived at the hairdresser's with a minute to spare and was happy to sit for a couple of hours and be offered a complimentary cappuccino. It was the only time I treated myself to this type of drink and I had been looking forward to the event. I had always had a reputation for being somewhat of a compulsive personality no matter what the activity or interest happened to be, therefore relaxing and doing nothing was a novelty. My colorist and I chatted about "nothings" as one does in these situations and she took a moment to bring me the cappuccino. I gratefully accepted and as I reached out from under the drop sheet, I was shocked to see that my left arm was completely bruised from elbow to wrist. Instinctively, I looked at my right arm, and there was bruising in the hand area, between my thumb and index finger. I felt a sickening flutter in my stomach and tried to calm myself. I knew that when I had walked into the hairdresser's my arms and hands were normal and now less than one hour later, out of nowhere, it looked like I had been in a fight with Mohammed Ali and lost! I was afraid to pick up and sip my coffee because I would be faced with looking at my arm again. Perhaps if I did not look at it, it would just go away. I sat there trying to rationalize it all. Surely, there had to be an explanation for this but for the life of me, I could not conjure up a good one. Having always been a logical person and in control of my emotions, I determined that this had to be something silly. I would just get my hair done and do some grocery shopping afterwards...life as usual.

When I got home, I unloaded the groceries and wondered what Bob would say about this inexplicable bruising? I reminded myself that I had never been sick a day in my life, had never had a fever, and rarely had contracted a cold. My life's mission had been to eat right, exercise and maintain a healthy weight. To our friends, I was known as the Energizer Esther Bunny! My girlfriends always used to joke about wanting some of what I had...little did they know that that would be the last thing they would want. Nothing serious could possibly be wrong with me, how could it, I had always done everything by the book. I proceeded to the last chore of the day which was to gather all the hoses from my daily watering. As I was reeling, I clipped the inside of my ankle and when I looked down, I was mortified to see that I was bleeding and that an area under the skin had bruised resembling one of those large, formless ink blotches used for personality testing. The bruise was spreading. Now I knew I could no longer ignore this and I had to seek medical attention immediately. I contacted the young girl who worked in our barn on weekends and told her I was taking myself to the hospital. She promised to feed and look after our dogs until I got home.

I drove to the hospital with the most profound dread in my gut. Denial was no longer working. Bob would not be home for another four hours…what a time to be alone! When I got to the emergency department, I completed the forms in triage and awaited a doctor. After an unbearably long hour, a doctor arrived and asked me what my problem was. I showed him my arms and ankle and told him the day's events and that I had no explanation for this bruising. I could tell that from years of dealing with situations like this, he immediately assumed some type of spousal abuse but went through the protocol nonetheless and ordered some blood tests. While I waited for the results, I phoned a friend who was picking Bob up at the airport and told him what was going on. I asked him not to mention anything to Bob about my afternoon at the hospital since I expected to be home and I did not want to alarm him unnecessarily.

I continued to wait and all sorts of things went through my mind, none of them good. I stared at the cement block walls, the ceiling, the floor and the clock. The minutes ticked by in slow motion. Finally, the doctor returned with my results and as I looked at his face, I knew I did not want to hear whatever it was he had to say. "Do you realize that if you were in a car accident right now, you would bleed to death?" he said. "Uh, no," I answered. He proceeded to tell me my blood results, which may as well have been Chinese for all the sense it made. I have become an expert on blood counts in the past six years, but at that time I was very ignorant. He informed me that my platelets (the part of your blood that stops you from bleeding to death) were virtually non-existent and that my white cells (basically your immune system that prevents you from getting sick) were close to nil. I had become a hemophiliac and "The Boy in the Bubble" all in one afternoon. As calmly as I could I asked him what was going on? He said that he was not an expert in hematology (the study of blood in short) but that an oncologist familiar with hematology was on call that night. The mere mention of that "oncology" word made me shudder. The only time I had dealt with that term was when Bob's mother had been diagnosed with lung cancer and the outcome of that scenario had not been pretty. He said I should get undressed and put a gown on so that I would be ready for an examination when the oncologist arrived. Why did I need to put a gown on I wondered?

Feeling lonely and terrified, I waited in one of the curtained cubicles. At one point, a nurse walked by and looked at me with what I viewed as excessive sympathy. She obviously knew something that I did not…in retrospect, ignorance truly is bliss. Within a short period of time, I started to shake non-stop and the nurse had to bring me a couple of blankets. I'll admit, it was cold there, but the shaking was from complete, unadulterated terror!

Another half-hour passed and then the oncologist arrived. I will refer to him as Dr. Personality because that is what he was NOT. He looked at the results of my blood tests and asked me a number of questions to do with my health and whether I was on any medications or supplements. I mentioned that I was taking nothing other than black cohosh and soy protein to help deal with hot flashes that had just started six months prior. I had turned 48 that year and was in the throes of perimenopause. He felt my neck and moved his hands to the glands in my throat. During all of this, he made no comments. Foolishly I said, "I had a mammogram five months ago," as if that somehow absolved me from whatever my current problem was. He stared at me with a look reserved for an idiot. You wonder why you say ridiculous things when you are under pressure. I decided to stay silent. Having concluded his exam he said as if to himself, that for some reason my bone marrow seemed to have stopped producing blood and related cells. I felt that I was having an out of body experience because I almost looked around the room to see whom he was speaking to. He stated that he would give me a prescription for a drug called prednisone which would hopefully kick-start my bone marrow into producing blood again. I asked him if I could go home, and he answered yes; however, he was going to schedule a bone marrow biopsy the following Tuesday and we would go from there. He advised me not to cut myself, not to get near anyone who was sick, or if I got a headache or fever to call the hospital pronto. If I knew then what I know now, I would have asked to be hospitalized immediately. To this day, I do not understand why this doctor released me from the hospital. After all, the triage doctor had just told me that I could bleed to death if I was in an accident not to mention the fact that I had no immune system and any germ could be my death sentence. Why was Dr. Personality telling me it was all right to go home, alone, and in a vehicle no less? I had always trusted the authority and knowledge of the medical system and thus, without question, I left the hospital and walked to my car. I realized afterwards that the bruising on my arms and hand had been caused by the mere effort of holding the electric shears I had used for trimming the bushes. If that happened to my arms, what else could rupture and hemorrhage internally?

People passed me by and I envied them going about their day as if nothing was wrong and here I was living proof that things could change in a nanosecond. Eerily, when I turned on the ignition, the radio came on playing the song "What a Difference a Day Makes." One minute my life was perfect and the next, so very, very wrong. I stopped at the drugstore and picked up the prednisone and hoped that this would work for whatever the hell was wrong with me.

I arrived home by 6:30 and was relieved that I had plenty of time to spare before Bob got home. He was due to land at 7:00 p.m. and I expected him home by about 8:30 or so. Our dogs were excited to see me and as I looked at their happy, naïve faces, I wished at that moment that I could be a dog...never having to worry about anything. Being human with intellect had its drawbacks.

I was still somewhat shaky from the whole experience and went to lie down on the bed. Dudley jumped up and cuddled in which relaxed me somewhat until I was startled by the ringing of the phone ...it was Bob calling from his cell on his way home. He sounded elated from his week of fishing and from the sound of his voice he couldn't wait to tell me about his experiences. After hearing me say hello, he immediately sensed that something was amiss. I guess you don't live with someone for 28 years and not know them inside out. Halfway through my explanation of having been at the hospital, the call was dropped. I was ready to scream in frustration. Within seconds, it rang again and I told Bob that I would explain everything when he got home. That was the longest hour of my life. When Bob got out of the car, he rushed towards me and held me with an intensity that can only come from knowing you may lose the person you love the most.

We sat in the family room and I described what had happened since early that morning. In a way, it felt like an eternity ago. The mention of a bone marrow biopsy filled us both with indescribable fear. We knew this was serious and we were clueless as to why this was happening to me. How could our normal lives be turned upside down by something so sudden and inexplicable? Because we had no concrete answers, we decided to keep this to ourselves until the outcome of the biopsy on

Tuesday. There was no point in telling anyone until we had some definitive answers. I was still hopeful for good news, although deep down I knew I was in trouble and didn't want to share that feeling.

For the next three days, I questioned every aspect of my life and I realized the signs had been there but I had chosen to ignore them. I had been tired during the summer but had attributed it to the heat, not to mention the fact that I was always on the go. I had bruised more often than usual but had not given it a second thought. After all, when one handled high-spirited horses, getting stepped on or jostled was all part of the equine experience. There was always a way to rationalize everything and I had done a great job of ignoring my body and what it was trying to tell me. I looked back at the preceding several months and thought about what had changed in my life. I had started taking black cohosh and soy protein and since those were the only two clues I had, I decided to get on the internet and see if anything negative came up relating to them. Soy seemed to have no bad press but when I began researching the black cohosh, I was shocked to find similar stories from people who had taken this herbal supplement. No one had died, but there were tales of people who had been admitted to the hospital for blood related issues that were similar to mine. Thankfully, the negative effects on the blood had been reversed once the person had stopped taking the cohosh. I printed off this material and felt that I had found a lifeline! Surely, Dr. Personality would welcome this research and I promptly called the hospital and asked for his fax number which they helpfully provided. After I faxed the information, I ran out to Bob and told him what I had found and he too felt renewed hope that there would be an end to this nightmare.

On Monday morning, the phone rang and it was Dr. Personality's office. The nurse was livid that I had the audacity to fax their office. She stated that the fax line was reserved for communication from doctors and medical personnel only. I was stunned at the brusqueness of this woman's voice. Didn't she understand that I was beside myself and needed something to give me a shred of hope? Feeling like a whipped puppy, I apologized and said that I would take the papers to him in the morning when I went in for the biopsy.

Tuesday arrived and Bob and I headed off to the hospital for our 10:00 a.m. appointment. We were silent in the car, each wrapped up in our own thoughts and worries. I had often wondered what it would be like to be able to read people's minds and came to the conclusion that it was best that we did not have that ability. When I arrived, I was asked to put on a hospital gown and a young nurse took Bob and me to a very sterile room to await the doctor. Why did all these rooms have to look like cement bunkers? She explained that she would stand by my side during the procedure and that Dr. Personality would insert a needle into my hipbone and take out a piece of bone marrow tissue for testing. After about an hour he arrived and I immediately told him about the research I had done and what I had found out about the black cohosh. As I reached out to give him the sheet, he dismissed it with a wave of his hand nearly hitting the paper. He said he had no interest in reading anything about herbal supplements and that anyone who took something like that without it being researched by a pharmaceutical company got what was coming to them. Those may not have been the exact words, but that was what he meant. I was shocked and felt like a severely scolded child. I knew it was all Bob could do not to punch said Doctor out! This man had zero sensitivity and I could not understand how he ended up in a profession whose ideology was to help and save people. He should have gone into research where all he dealt with were inanimate objects such as Petri dishes, glass vials and microscopes.

Dr. Personality began to explain what he would be doing and then looked at Bob in a condescending fashion and suggested that he leave the room saying that most observers normally passed out from watching the procedure. All I could think was, if he's worried about Bob passing out, what about me!!?? Bob glared at him, struggling to keep his quick temper under control answering that he would be fine and would stay with me. I knew Bob could handle it because he had experienced many injuries himself from training horses to jump; things like broken ribs, dislocated shoulder and fractured vertebrae. He was one tough cookie but this would be the first time that the shoe was on the other foot as it were.

I was lying on the bed face down and the nurse took my hand. I was perplexed as to why she had done this. It never occurred to me that this was going to be the most excruciating pain I had ever experienced in my life. Bob told me later that the needle that was used was extremely long and had a very wide end – much larger even than any needle we had ever used on one of our horses. I'm glad I didn't see that before Dr. Personality started. He disinfected the skin on my hip with alcohol and gave me an injection to freeze the area.

He warned me he was about to start with the biopsy needle which would be painful and that he would understand if I started to yell. Excuse me? The lights were going on as to why the nurse was holding my hand. He inserted the needle and as he got closer to the bone, the pain intensified to about an eight on the Richter scale. We hit TEN when he began to use the needle like a jackhammer into my hipbone. I felt as if I was being driven through the mattress. With his entire body weight behind him, Dr. Personality was pumping the needle trying to get into the bone to get to the soft section within, the marrow. The pain was like nothing I had ever felt. With each blow to my hip, I was squeezing the nurse's hand harder and harder. I was determined not to scream…I would not give Dr. Personality that satisfaction.

The torture finally ceased, or so I thought, only to be told that he had not gotten in deep enough and would have to start anew. I kept thinking…why is this happening to me? I must have been a really bad person in a previous life. I grabbed the nurse's hand and the needle was again inserted. At last he stopped and said he had enough marrow. He stitched up the incision because he was worried about excessive bleeding due to my low platelet count and then complimented me on my toughness and said few people made it through without crying out. I derived some pleasure from that comment. As I turned around to look at him, I noticed that his shirt was wet with perspiration. I guess he had his workout for the day at my expense.

Dr. Personality said he would have the results in two days, Thursday, September 1st, and he would make an appointment to give us the news. He also mentioned that the medication I had been taking since my emergency room visit had done nothing to improve my bone marrow function based on the blood analysis he had done that morning. Now it was a "wait and see" game until Thursday. I went into the bathroom to get changed and realized that the back of my underwear was drenched in blood. The nurse found me some paper underwear and I got dressed.

I was thankful that the car was parked close to the hospital, because at this point I felt like my body had been hit by a truck. The drive home was silent and I was once again thankful that we could not read each other's thoughts.

It is difficult to explain what it was like emotionally for both of us the ensuing two days. Bob continued to look after our farm, property and our retail business and I was doing small house chores. I began to feel very weak; obviously, the bone marrow biopsy had literally been "the straw that broke the camel's back." We tried to have a feeling of normalcy in our lives, but deep down the panic we felt went beyond words. I was literally going through the day in a robotic kind of trance. At night we would hold each other in bed and hope that things were going to be all right. Bob had always been a very strong person used to being in charge of his life and destiny; this situation of being powerless and not in control was an unwelcome, foreign feeling to him.

Wednesday brought a pleasant, superficial diversion to our worries. Three of Bob's old-time buddies came to celebrate one of them retiring. This had been planned weeks ahead with a dinner at a nearby restaurant and an overnight stay at our house and we did not have the heart to cancel the evening. We tried to have fun but there was an ominous feeling in the air and it was difficult to pretend that nothing was wrong. We knew that Thursday was looming ahead and we couldn't shake our apprehension for whatever news was to come.

Chapter 2
September 1ˢᵗ to September 4ᵗʰ

In the morning, Jim, Eric and Danny left early and said they would be in touch later on to find out the results from my biopsy. Their concern was touching. At about 9:00 a.m., I received a call from the doctor's office advising us that he was running late and would not be able to see us until 12:30 p.m. Great. The torment of the unknown would be prolonged for another few hours. Would this uncertainty and emotional agony ever end? As it turned out, we were barely at the tip of the iceberg for what lay ahead of us.

With lead in our feet, we got in the car and drove to the hospital. We had been informed to go to the oncology department and wait near the day-care room which was where out-patients received their chemotherapy treatments and blood product transfusions. What was I doing here I kept asking myself? Bob and I made idle chit chat and frankly, I don't think either of us even knew what we were saying. For the first time in our lives we were faced with a view of a world we had never seen before...people dying or, more aptly put, trying their damnedest not to die. I was asked to fill out a 12-page form which asked the same tedious questions that I had already answered prior to my biopsy procedure. I later learned that often the right hand did not know what the left hand was doing.

After what seemed like an eternity, we were finally called into Dr. Personality's small examination room. It was as impersonal as he was with not a single family photograph in sight. Why did that not surprise me? Bob and I sat adjacent to each other, I with my back against the wall as if its hardness would somehow give me emotional fortitude. We both felt we would explode from the waiting and tension. Dr. Personality came in, sat down and looked only at me said, "Well, I don't have good news – it looks like you have a disease called Aplastic Anemia." I did not have a clue what he was talking about. I remember thinking, OK, give me some medication and I'm sure I'll be fine...I just want my life back as it was.

Seeing the blank look on my face, he gave us a brief description of this illness. He described aplastic anemia as a blood disorder, like leukemia and other such cancers, but it was, in fact, not cancer. Essentially, for some unknown reason, my bone marrow had died and thus ceased producing blood. "Aplastic" is a derivative of the word aplasia, meaning lack of development of an organ or tissue. I did not know much, but I knew you could not be without this vital production for long. Bob and I did not look at each other – we couldn't. The doctor seemed to wait for either of us to say something. Keeping my emotions under control, I asked what I should be asking or doing at this point? He said that there was no cure other than a bone marrow transplant but there was the possibility of undergoing some type of chemical therapy to prolong my life *if I was not already in the advanced stages of the disease.* Again I was back to where I felt like I was listening to Chinese. He offered to call McMaster University Hospital the following Tuesday and make an appointment for me within a couple of weeks. I was aware of McMaster, which was about a 45-minute drive away. Slowly my brain was digesting this information and I came to the realization that "no cure" meant I was going to die! One always wonders what one's reaction will be in a situation such as this when you are told you have limited time left in this world. This is how I coped with the news: Bob told me later that my eyes rolled up into my head, I went into some kind of seizure and promptly hit the back of my skull against the cement wall behind me and passed out. About 10 minutes later, I woke up on the floor with a cold compress on my forehead and no Dr. Personality in sight. My dislike of this man was increasing by the minute. Bob looked down at me with such worry in his eyes it made me want to cry. I felt like I had been hit by lightning – maybe that would have been more merciful! Every ounce of energy and strength had been zapped from my body. The nurse who was holding the compress asked me if I was able to get up. At this point, Dr. Personality stuck his head in the door to see if I was still alive, no doubt worried that I was going to sue him for damages. I looked at him and said I was fine. When I got up, my legs were shaking so badly that I told Bob I didn't think I could walk out of the hospital. The nurse quickly volunteered to get someone to take me to the parking area in a wheelchair…my first of many such wheelchair rides. Today was September 1, 2005. I suddenly remembered this was our 29th wedding anniversary…some anniversary.

Bob feeling much like me but being the strong force that he was, went to get the car and met me in the parking area. The volunteer who wheeled me downstairs listened sympathetically while I told her what had happened. I must say that the following months exposed us to many doctors, nurses and volunteers and 99% of them were angels sent from heaven. Thankfully, I would no longer be dealing with that one percent that was Dr. Personality.

We drove home trying to grasp what we had been told and thinking how we were going to deal with this shocking news. When we had settled into our family room about an hour later, we began to talk about a game plan. Bob felt that waiting for an appointment "within two weeks" at McMaster University Hospital was just too far down the road for something this serious. There was no option other than to take matters into our own hands and Bob decided to phone very good friends of ours in Ohio who were doctors at one of the top clinics in the U.S.A. Surely, they would be able to guide us in terms of what to do. Bob left a message for Janet and when she returned his call, he told her about my diagnosis of aplastic anemia. Needless to say she was taken aback as was everyone when they heard the news. Janet agreed with Bob that two weeks was too long to wait and she asked if we could be prepared to come to Ohio the following Tuesday which was five days away. She apologized that no physicians would be available until then due to the September long weekend. We determined that was better than waiting two weeks and considering how I felt, the sooner the better. Janet advised Bob that he would need to get my medical records and the actual biopsy specimen from Dr. Personality. Bob planned on phoning the hospital with that request the next day, which was Friday. We would head to Ohio on Monday and be ready for my appointment on Tuesday. After he hung up the phone, we felt better that at least we were somewhat in control of our destiny again.

Not able to put the inevitable off any longer, it was time to call my family and tell them the awful news. I have a small family, just my mother and brother, Pat, and sister-in-law, Linda. We decided to phone Pat first. He was shocked to hear what we had been going through and asked us to keep him up to date with every detail. The next call was to my Mom. Bob would do all the talking because frankly, I was unable to communicate with anyone both from a physical and emotional standpoint. I felt badly for Mom because I knew she was on Cloud 9 in anticipation of her older sister flying in from Belgium the following afternoon. She had been looking forward to her arrival for weeks and in typical Belgian fashion, Mom had been cooking and cleaning for days on end. Talk about bursting her euphoric bubble! Mom was 73 at that time and this was not the kind of news we wanted to relay but we had no choice. I'm not sure to this day whether Mom really understood the severity of what she was told. Imagine being ecstatically happy one moment and then finding out your daughter has a rare, terminal illness. I do not think that a parent can cope psychologically with the news that there is a high likelihood that their child is going to die before them. It is not in the natural order of things. After Bob hung up, we chatted a while longer about our plan for Ohio.

The following morning, Bob got the ball rolling to get my records and biopsy specimen. The Canadian medical system is not very willing to give you your own information and after much shouting and threatening they complied and Bob was able to pick up everything that afternoon. While I was at home, my health was getting worse by the minute. It had only been 24 hours since I had been diagnosed but each hour brought with it more exhaustion and difficulty in breathing. Eventually, I learned that this was due to a low red blood cell count. Because I had always been one of those people to push on regardless of how I felt, I had not noticed my declining health. Now, the illness had reached the stage where it was taking control of me and I could not believe how weak I felt. I could not get out of bed…something that had never happened to me before. I had not been able to empathize when people said they were so feeble that they could barely move but now I understood. I vowed that if I survived, I would have a more open-minded perspective towards things I had not personally experienced.

In a matter of days, I had gone from worrying about nothing to worrying about absolutely everything. Dr. Personality had advised us to take my temperature regularly because the appearance of a fever could prove dangerous if not deadly since I had no immune system. We had to be vigilant to catch that in time. And then there was, of course, the added bonus of my newfound hemophiliac status and having to make sure I didn't cut myself or get in an accident. I felt like my body was a ball in a pinball machine game being launched from one threat to the next. To say that I was petrified didn't even come close to describing my feelings.

As I steadily became weaker, Bob began making my meals and looked after everything in the house from laundry to cleaning to watering my 100 or so plants. As if he didn't have enough to do with his regular duties. How could my life be reduced to being bedridden in such a short period of time? We had always joked that he was the outdoor slave and I was the indoor slave. We each did what we did best and neither of us viewed our roles as being sexist. Bob looked after the property and maintenance of it, as well as the big picture relating to our retail business and I was the detail person handling the bookkeeping, housekeeping and finesse landscaping. We were a team: we worked and played together. Our relationship had begun when I was 19 and Bob, 29. Communication had always been the biggest plus of our marriage – that, and a sense of humor. Bob said he could make me laugh regardless of the circumstance and he was right. Before dinner each night, we would sit for a couple hours with a glass of our favorite California Chardonnay and discuss daily events, philosophies and life in general. Don't get me wrong, our marriage was not perfect but when we did have arguments we solved them through open communication. We knew we were lucky in that regard. I think this strong foundation is what helped us cope with such an extraordinary challenge. The pressure on Bob to deal with everything was mammoth, and to this day I don't know how he did it.

By Saturday I had absolutely no strength; in fact, I barely had enough breath to talk on the phone. Under normal conditions, Bob would have made a joke about me not being able to speak but humor was not part of his persona these days. Everything was a giant effort for my body. I lay in bed with the windows open and I could hear Bob mowing the lawn and doing his outside jobs. At one point, I heard the woeful cries of a gaggle of geese flying overhead and wondered if I would see the fall of 2006? My world was now reduced to the four walls of our bedroom and the only connection to the outside was what I could hear beyond our window. So many thoughts went through my mind. I was completely drained yet I could not sleep. I started writing down all of the things that I did in relation to our bookkeeping that Bob had never done. After all, if I didn't make it he would have to know how I dealt with our bill payments, banking and such. I even worried about our income tax returns and getting them done. Talk about crazy! Here I was facing death and I was concerned with stupid, meaningless tasks. It is difficult to change who you are and I was damned if I was going to die and leave a disorganized mess behind. Unbeknownst to Bob, I wrote a letter making provisions in the eventuality that I died and hid it in my lingerie drawer. I emailed Leslie, a long-time girlfriend of 30 years and told her what I had done. I asked her to advise Bob of the letter when the time came. Over six years later, the letter still remains in my drawer. I am afraid to throw it away.

To keep me from going stir-crazy, Bob had set up portable speakers in our bedroom so that I could listen to our favorite radio stations. We had always loved music and especially instrumentals. In fact, I had taken up classical guitar lessons five years prior. I had barely even scratched the surface of becoming an accomplished musician and it seemed I would never get the chance to continue my musical quest. As I listened to the radio, songs that I had heard before had a completely new meaning. What I had perceived as being buoyant and joyful in the past, now struck me as sad and melancholy. At one point, a song came on that I had never heard before, by a Hawaiian singer named Israel Kamakawiwo'le. It was a medley but was based mainly on "Somewhere Over the Rainbow." The poignant lyrics of the song said everything that I felt and, listening to it, I decided that this was the song I wanted played at my funeral. It wasn't that I was jumping the gun but I had always been a realist and planning for my funeral seemed the logical thing to do. My motto had always been "Be prepared." When I hear this song nowadays, I still get a tightening in my stomach.

Many close friends called over that two-day period and Bob had to talk to them all because I couldn't. With each call, Bob had to go through the entire explanation again and on many occasions had to hang up because he would get choked up. By the end of Saturday, I was so weak that Bob had to help me shower. It seemed I had become an invalid instantly. Only two days had passed since our meeting at the hospital, but somehow each day felt like five because of the escalation of my deteriorating health. Bob made me dinner and sat next to my bed while I tried to force some food down. Unfortunately, I had always been one of those people that when stressed, I could not eat. I just about choked on each mouthful. I knew that not eating would only worsen my predicament and I persevered until most of the meal was gone.

Sunday came and I felt worse than the day before. I decided that at this rate, I would be a corpse by the time Tuesday rolled around. While Bob was outside, I phoned our friend Janet and told her how I was feeling. She said she would consult someone in their hematology section and get back to me. When she phoned, she said the doctor felt that it would be unsafe for me to come to Ohio in my current condition and that I should get to a hospital immediately. Their hematologist was worried that if we were in a serious car accident en route to Ohio, I would die from blood loss. Bob was back in the house at this point and also talked with Janet and they both agreed I needed to get medical care ASAP. We decided to call an ambulance and head for McMaster University Hospital ourselves, medical records in hand, and go to their emergency room. While we were waiting for the ambulance, Bob, knowing he was in no shape to drive our car, phoned Mike to ask if he would be able to. Mike said he would be there post-haste. We quickly threw some things in a bag for me and as Bob was getting organized, I grabbed a post-it note and wrote "I love you" on it and placed it on his pillow. I honestly didn't know how long I would be alive and if I would even be coming back to this house at all. The Post-It Note to this day, sticks to our bedroom mirror.

When the ambulance arrived, Bob showed the attendants into the bedroom and while they were taking my vitals, he told them we needed to go to McMaster. They looked at Bob and said that they were not allowed to take us to a hospital outside of their jurisdiction and that we had to go to the local one. Having already been there for my biopsy and initial emergency-room visit, we knew that they could not offer us what we needed. The ambulance drivers were genuinely sorry and suggested we call a private, patient transfer company that could take us anywhere we wanted. By this time, Mike had arrived and the decision was made to forget the transfer and Mike would drive us in our car. While Mike and I were seated in the car waiting for Bob to close the garage doors, I turned to him and said, "I don't know if I'm going to "make it," would you please make sure that Bob gets through this after I'm gone." He looked at me shocked and answered that I would make it and not to say such things. I had said my piece and that was what mattered.

Once at the hospital, Bob found a wheelchair and took me into the emergency room. Sadly my wheelchair trips seemed to be becoming a regular thing. It occurred to me that several times in my life I had dreamt about being in a wheelchair and this seemed strangely prophetic. Bob had been advised by Janet to tell the admitting nurse that I was Neutropenic, which means you have no immune system. The last thing we wanted was to be in an emergency room with a bunch of germ-laden people and me with no way of fighting anything off. When the triage nurse took our information, Bob told her about my illness and she had us wait in a small room that was sectioned off from the general public in the emergency-room area. This type of problem is not taken lightly by anyone with medical knowledge. After a brief waiting period, a young doctor arrived and we explained my background including our idea about the side effects of the black cohosh I had been taking for three months.

The doctor was quite sympathetic and surprised that we had my medical records, not to mention the biopsy itself, in our possession. We told him we had all of this because we had been planning to go to Ohio but that due to my worsening condition, we had changed our plans. When he viewed my records, he understood that I was not your run-of-the-mill emergency-room patient with a sprained ankle or cracked rib. He decided to do additional blood tests and a nurse came by to insert my first IV to draw blood. I had always been squeamish about blood and could virtually pass out from the sight of it, so I pinched my thumb and looked the other way to distract myself from what she was doing. For this reason I had never donated blood and I have regretted that on many occasions. After my blood was drawn, we were told that one of the top hematologists in their hospital was on call that night, and that she would be contacted to come and see us. We felt that our problems would be solved…we were in a top-notch hospital about to be seen by a renowned specialist. Naïvely, we still hoped that if the black cohosh was the cause of my illness, these professionals would figure out some way of reversing the effects. Bob and I waited in yet another small, cement room, holding hands and oh so very frightened…he, of losing me, and me of losing him… and me!

Two hours later, a hematologist named Dr. Parveen Wasi came in to see us. She was of slight build with a warm smile…not at all what we had expected…Dr. Personality was still too fresh in our memory banks. Dr. Wasi introduced herself and said the emergency doctor had apprised her of my condition but would we please go over the details again with her. We were more than happy to explain it once more and when we finished we looked at her hopefully. She said she understood that even though we thought that the cohosh might have been a factor, the bottom line was that once the bone marrow stopped functioning, there was no reversal. I had secretly hoped that there would be a magic potion to be consumed and all would be well again, but that would have been too simple. Dr. Wasi said that based on the results of the blood they had taken I would be admitted to their blood disorder ward immediately. She informed us that if Dr. Personality's findings were correct, then a bone marrow transplant was the only viable option for a cure. Dr. Wasi asked if I had any siblings that could be tested as potential donors and I told her I only had one brother. Luckily at that time, I had no idea what little hope there was for a single sibling to be a match. She requested his name and personal contact information so that her transplant team could get in touch with him quickly and arrange for him to be tested. The fact that she was already asking for these details left me with little doubt as to the urgency in finding a donor. Bob and I looked at each other with some relief that at least I would be in professional medical hands now…not that we had a clue what that would entail. We thanked Dr. Wasi and she left.

At this point, it was late evening and Mike had been in the emergency waiting-room all this time. It was decided that Bob and Mike would go home since our dogs needed to be looked after. Bob kissed me and left. I could see he had the weight of the world on his shoulders. As for me, I sat there and waited for the next step. I had seen more hospitals and examination rooms in the past week than in my entire life. After about an hour, an orderly arrived with a stretcher and I was wheeled to a room on the third floor in Ward 3Z, the blood disorder section. A nurse came in and helped transfer me to the bed. We once again went through countless questions and answers. When we finished, I noticed that these were all private rooms, with curtains drawn across the windows that faced the hallway. I realized that once you "made it" to these rooms it was because you could not be in contact with anyone else for fear of catching something. What a lonely disease this was…just when you needed people around you the most, you could not be with them because their germs could be your demise.

With the nurse's assistance, I changed into a hospital gown and kept feeling that this could not possibly be happening to me. I had never been in a hospital overnight and I felt so frightfully alone. My nurse, Leah, was wonderful and she tried to make me feel better, difficult as that was. She showed me where the bell was that would alert the nurse's station if I needed anything and I felt a little peculiar at the thought of using a buzzer to summon someone. I felt that that should have been reserved for royalty or the likes of the rich and famous. After she left, I turned out the lights and eventually fell into a troubled sleep. Throughout my life, I have always been a heavy dreamer and much to Bob's chagrin I could usually remember every detail of my typically bad dreams. I could have written science fiction or horror novels based on some of the dreams I had. This night was no exception. I dreamt that I was asleep and struggling with wet clothing. When I looked down, I was covered in blood and I realized I was bleeding to death! I tried to breathe and could not for the blood I was choking on. I woke up in a panic and sat bolt upright. My hospital gown was soaked in sweat and I was hyperventilating from the sheer terror of it all. I tried to regain some composure. Ever since I had been diagnosed four days prior, my greatest fear had been of bleeding to death, which had now manifested itself in this horrific nightmare. Still gasping for air, I rang for the nurse…so much for thinking I would never ring the bell. When Leah arrived I asked her for a fresh hospital gown. She looked at me with such compassion in her eyes…probably because we were close to the same age and that philosophy of "There but for the grace of God go I" went through her mind. She turned her back to me as I changed out of the wet gown, which frankly surprised me. I learned that the nurses always did their utmost to respect your privacy. I barely slept the remainder of the night and morning finally dawned.

Chapter 3
September 5ᵗʰ to September 7ᵗʰ

At 8:00 a.m. breakfast arrived, termed loosely and living up to typical hospital food. The coffee tasted like brown swill, a stale muffin graced the plate and alongside sat a cup of yogurt. The good news was that the hospital cafeteria had read my dietary requirement sheet which stated that I was a vegetarian and if nothing else, this meal certainly was that. I had been a vegetarian for 18 years and had chosen this lifestyle because of my love for animals. I was steadfast in my dedication but not fanatical. If all there was left on this earth was meat, I would have eaten that to survive. Given the fact there were still choices, I chose not to eat animals. I've been surprised and disappointed numerous times these past few years by seemingly intelligent people who assumed that the "anemia" part of the aplastic anemia was due to a low iron count and they consequently attributed my illness to being a vegetarian. Hopefully, my story will dispel these misconceptions.

By nine o'clock, Bob walked into the room. I had never been happier at seeing anyone in my life…he was in fact, my life! We hugged and could barely let go of each other. I asked him how things were at home with the dogs and horses and I was glad to hear that everything was under control there. Bob decided that he would stay until noon and then return in the afternoon and stay overnight in my room. The nurses had told him they would find a cot for him to sleep on. I was comforted with this news. The nursing staff bent over backwards in order to bring some happiness and comfort to their patients.

Because it was Labor Day Monday, we did not see Dr. Wasi that day, but things were going on behind the scenes that we did not know about. Bob left at midday and I was left in my solitude. I knew that Mom, Pat and Linda were worried sick but because I had no strength, I couldn't even call them. Bob had promised to be my liaison and would keep in touch with them on a daily basis.

The day passed with some rapidity. Nurses came in regularly to take my blood pressure, temperature and oxygen levels. At precisely noon, lunch arrived. It was a good thing I had not been waiting with bated breath. Under the metal cover was a lukewarm piece of ham alongside gluey, mashed potatoes that resembled plaster of Paris. Obviously, the hospital kitchen had mislaid the paperwork as to my vegetarian status. It wasn't really a loss for two reasons: number one, I had no appetite; and number two, I was developing some nasty mouth sores because my immune system was shutting down. I had found out that when your white cells (leukocytes) disappear, your body begins to "infect" itself because it can no longer fight its own bacteria. I was informed that your mouth is the most bacteria laden part of your body, which is why for the most part, kissing a dog is actually safer than kissing another human being's mouth. Disinterestedly, I picked away at the mashed potatoes.

At about 2:00 p.m., a resident hematologist made rounds and I asked her if she had any updates for me. I'm sure she was knowledgeable and efficient, but her bedside manner left a lot to be desired…perhaps she was a distant relative of Dr. Personality? She advised me that I was scheduled for yet another biopsy the next day and I nearly passed out at that news. The very thought of having that repeated sent me into a panic. I still had significant pain and bruising from the last ordeal. I would tell Bob as soon as he arrived and I hoped that he would be able to dissuade them from that procedure. Why did they need another biopsy when we had given them the one taken by Dr. Personality? In the meantime, I amused myself by listening to the radio having no interest whatsoever in watching TV...it all seemed so meaningless in light of what I was facing. Who needed to watch a bunch of screaming contestants or yet another episode of "CSI?" Music was my solace.

Sometime in the afternoon, a male nurse came in holding some papers. He introduced himself as Gavin and immediately commented that he found it unusual that I was listening to the radio as opposed to watching TV. I gathered not too many patients went the music route favoring television. Gavin agreed with my choice saying that he preferred music as well. I happened to be lying on the bed cross-legged and he suggested I straighten out my legs because I could get a blood clot. There I was in the pinball machine again, being flung to the "Blood Clot" sign. He explained he had brought in two sets of sheets that covered in detail everything I needed to know about my disease. To this day, I find it strange that no one in the hospital actually sat me down and told me what aplastic anemia was all about...face to face, Mano a Mano. I think in their defense it is because in a system of socialized medicine as is the case in Canada, the doctors and nurses are so overworked that there is just no time for the personal touch and besides, reading official, documented research leaves no room for error in the patient's understanding of what is happening to them. Once Gavin left, I looked at the papers as if they were rattlesnakes about to strike. Hesitantly, I picked them up and began to read. I think I made it through to the third page and stopped reading, setting the whole thing aside. I didn't need to know any more. This was an exceptionally rare disease and afflicted only one in a million people. Based on the population of the U.S.A., a mere 450 people acquired this disease annually. No wonder I had never heard of it. My mother had always said I was special but this special, I did not need to be. I learned that based on my blood results, I was in the "severe to very severe stage" of aplastic anemia. Because I was in the worst stage, the chances for survival were small and the only choice I had was a bone marrow transplant…which by the way, had to be done in about four weeks. It was a do-or-die scenario! I further read that the older you were, the less chance you had of surviving the transplant. I didn't think I was "old" at 48, but the older you are the riskier the procedure and the less able your body is to accept another person's marrow. I guess if I had been a teenager or in my twenties, things would have looked better. In terms of the bone marrow matching, I had two choices: a match from a sibling (which was the ideal scenario) and failing that, a worldwide search would be made for a match from a non-related donor, which could present more negative side effects. To make matters worse, the likelihood of a sibling being a match was extremely remote. Given that I only had my one brother Pat, I guessed that the percentages were even lower than winning a lottery. I wished at that moment that I wasn't as good at calculating numbers. How bleak this all seemed!

As for the details of the disease, I also learned that 50% of the people are diagnosed as having "Idiopathic" aplastic anemia, meaning that the cause of the disease is unknown. The remaining percentage is diagnosed as having "Acquired" aplastic anemia where specific external factors may have contributed to the person developing the disease. Such things as high doses of radiation, certain chemotherapies, insecticides, chemicals, specific medications, exposure to benzene and some viruses could cause the disease in some people. I tried to think about what could have caused mine and wondered whether the black cohosh was indeed the culprit. No one in the medical community had any documentation on a link between the two. Since my transplant, I periodically check the internet for new information relating to the causes of aplastic anemia. Interestingly, a doctor wrote a paper about a patient who had been taking black cohosh in combination with soy supplements. Apparently, in her research, the two in specific dosages were a toxic duo. Looking back, other possibilities surface…I innocently or stupidly exposed myself to the careless use of household cleaning chemicals and the icing on the cake was probably the black cohosh and soy. Not once did I read a label to see whether I should be inhaling or touching any of the products that I used…for as much as I looked after myself from a diet and exercise standpoint, I was completely oblivious to the dangers of cleaning products. The bottom line is: I will never know. As they say…too late smart. I was one of the unlucky few to be susceptible to this bombardment of chemicals and/or supplements and it destroyed the function of my bone marrow.

As I was thinking, Gavin came in to chat. He seemed like such a nice man as was everyone in that ward…all so empathetic and in spite of their surroundings, they were always upbeat. Frankly, I didn't know how they managed it. He asked me if there were any questions and I said I had none. The information had been very thorough; too thorough in fact. I did ask him why I was to have another biopsy taken the following day since they already had the original specimen. Gavin answered that it would actually be a bone marrow aspiration that would take fluid out, as opposed to a "piece" of marrow, which had been the purpose of the initial biopsy. The aspiration would be less painful. That was at least a teeny bit of good news. They needed more fluid to be able to do further tests. I guess there was no escaping another needle being jabbed into my hipbone…in a way, I was already getting used to being poked and prodded. Having covered everything, Gavin said goodbye and that he would see me later.

Bob returned to the hospital at about 5:00 p.m. and he had brought a small cooler with some of our favorite chardonnay.

This was contraband but what the heck, even if I didn't feel like any, he might as well have some. I certainly felt that he deserved it! On his way in, he had stopped at the cafeteria and picked up a personal-sized pizza for himself and there he sat, having chardonnay out of a leftover plastic juice cup and eating pizza out of a cardboard box. What a change this was to our normal lifestyle! It's not that we were adverse to pizza, it was actually our favorite food, but it would have at least been eaten from a porcelain plate and the wine poured in a nice glass. As Bob was eating, my supper arrived and for a change, I was pleasantly surprised. Dinner was an East Indian lentil dish which was delightfully spicy and tasty. I noted with interest that it was outsourced to a caterer, as opposed to being prepared in the hospital, which certainly explained why it was so good. I was able to eat in reasonable comfort because the nurses had given me a liquid that you swished in your mouth prior to eating to freeze your gums and mouth tissue for a few minutes. That way, you wouldn't feel any pain while you were eating. The only thing the nurses did warn me about was to be careful that I didn't swallow any because it would freeze your throat and that was a "no-no." The liquid was appropriately called "Swish and Spit."

Bob and I talked about my first 24 hours in the hospital and that we did not know any more about what was going to happen with me than the day before. Since this was all so new to us, we just waited for people to tell us something...we had not gotten to the pro-active stage...yet. I told him about my chat with Gavin and the bone marrow aspiration scheduled for the next day. Bob was relieved that at least it wouldn't be as painful as the biopsy... ditto. At one point, I handed him the documentation on THE DISEASE and Bob basically did what I did which was to put it down after three pages. Neither of us really wanted to discuss it. Reading detail after detail only distressed us further and we felt that it was counterproductive to get bogged down by the negativity…we would just deal with whatever was thrown at us.

After a couple of hours, the nurses brought in the fold-up bed and in order to have a semblance of privacy, we dimmed the lights. Bob made up the bed with the sheets they had brought. I thought about the fact that the last time Bob had made a bed himself was in his bachelor days. He was completely out of his element and I kept thinking that I could have made the cot in two minutes. It was depressing to watch him. The gloomy lighting and surroundings made it all the more dismal. How could our lives change to this extent in a matter of just nine days and to such a subterranean depth? By the time Bob finished making up his cot we decided to call it a night. We were emotionally and physically exhausted and perhaps sleep would bring escape.

I learned that night that you do not sleep in a hospital, at least not in that ward anyway. The blood disorder ward mostly housed people with various types of leukemia and the odd aplastic anemia patient like me. By the time you got to that ward, you were either really sick or you had just undergone a bone marrow transplant and were in isolation. There were only about 12-15 patients in that ward at any one time but they were all in need of constant care. If the IV machines weren't beeping, someone needed their oxygen checked, or someone was throwing up. You get the picture. A lot of the patients looked like Auschwitz victims in the last stages of dying and inevitably that is what some of them did. Sometime during the night, we heard a loud buzzer go off and the sound of people running. We later found out that when that happened, there was usually an empty bed the following morning.

Tuesday morning came early and not so bright. My wake-up call was a needle poked into my arm. Part of the routine was for the nurses to take your blood at about 5:30 a.m. so that it could be sent to the lab before it opened to the public at 8:00 a.m. Your blood results would be back by 9:00 a.m. and then they would know whether you needed any hemoglobin or platelet transfusions that day. The complete blood chemistry also told them whether your kidneys and liver were functioning properly. I was in awe of the fact that a few vials of blood could tell just about everything to do with your health or in my case… non-health. I have to say that most of the nurses did an excellent job of inserting a needle with barely even a hint of pain.

Once the nurse left, Bob got up and un-made the cot and put everything together so that it could be used again that night. It brought great comfort to both of us that he was able to stay in the evenings. We were fortunate in that we had a support system that looked after our farm and its needs that enabled Bob to be with me. Many people were not that lucky. I guess there were some positives if you looked hard enough and I had always been the type to view the glass as half full as opposed to half empty. Lately though that philosophy had not been that easy to maintain.

Soon it was close to breakfast time, 8:00 a.m., and Bob left for home to get on with his daily jobs. He was awfully tired from having had next to no sleep and I could see the weariness in his face. Bob kissed me and said he would be back in the afternoon…same time, same channel. Shortly after he left, the resident hematologist arrived with a nurse I had not yet met. She said they were going to do the aspiration procedure and that I should lie on my stomach. I was getting to know this "drill" (pardon the pun) and didn't like it one little bit. This time, the nurse stayed with the hematologist in order to assist her and there was no offer of any handholding here. They suggested I hold the railing of the bed if I needed to. I guess I was becoming a veteran at this and they figured I didn't need the TLC any longer. As in the biopsy procedure, the skin was frozen and then a long, thinner needle was inserted into my hipbone. Let me tell you that although they had said it would be a good deal less painful, I can vouch that it was only slightly so. After a few minutes, the resident had the fluid she needed and said they were done. I had broken into a significant sweat from the pain. I smiled and jokingly said that if I had known I was going to perspire this much, I would have put on my heavy-duty deodorant. It was an attempt at humor, but neither cracked a smile. They were not used to someone making a joke under these circumstances.

Shortly after, a woman about my age came in for a visit. She had short gray hair and was wearing a black turtleneck and midi-length black skirt. I determined that she was a female Chaplain and things must be really bad if they had sent her to see me. Hopefully she wasn't here to read me my last rights! I was a bit on the defensive because neither Bob nor I were religious and I did not want someone trying to convert me at this late stage of the game. At times I wished I could have believed in the Hereafter but my logical mind could not comprehend that if there was a God, how could He sit idly by while humans destroyed each other and their environment? I did not want to get into an ideological conversation at this point. Our personal "religion" had always been to live honestly and justly and then everything else will fall into place…so much for that theory.

Within a few minutes, I realized that Maggie was a social worker and provided services for the patients in 3Z. Inwardly I breathed a sigh of relief. One of her functions was to arrange such things as governmental financial assistance for the dreadfully costly prescription drugs that many of these patients needed and could not afford. I was relieved that I was not in that position. Maggie was a marvelous listener and we started to talk about my illness and circumstance. I had a lot of time to think while I was in the hospital and I had realized that my greatest anguish was the thought of Bob being left alone if I died. We had never had children and Bob was rarely in touch with his sister, the only surviving member of his family. I pictured him alone in our house wandering from room to room without a soul to talk to other than our two dogs, Dudley and Max. Of course we had wonderful friends but everyone had their own lives and problems and at the end of the day, you were by yourself. I mentioned this to Maggie and she listened attentively but did not say much…that was her role. She had met countless patients in this ward and learned of their families, their lives and their tragedies. Basically, she had seen it all or most of it anyway. I think that is why she knew better than to voice meaningless platitudes. Maggie was aware of what I was facing and that the odds were stacked against me. She did ask if I wanted to speak to someone my age that had undergone a transplant or if Bob would want to speak to a fellow "caregiver." That was a new term for me, one that I had never heard before. I answered that at this time I didn't wish to speak to a fellow transplant patient. Truthfully, I did not want to know the details of what was ahead of me. I just wanted the big picture and besides, one person's experience is never the same as another's. I wanted to go into this with my own resolve and no preconceived negatives. As for Bob, he was not a "touchy-feely" guy and would not want to share his feelings with strangers. I politely declined on both counts. Maggie took no offense and said that should we change our minds, she could arrange a meeting for either Bob or me. I thanked her and she left saying that if there was anything I needed to please contact her. She was – and is – a lovely lady.

That day was busy in terms of things coming together. Kathy and Tina, two women that made up the transplant co-ordination unit, came to see me because they needed more information about my brother. They told me that they had been in touch with Pat and that he was going to be tested that very day. The results would take about a fortnight. Being so ignorant, I thought that this meant he would need to have a bone marrow aspiration done but all that was required was to have eight vials of blood taken. Nowadays a simple cheek swab can catalogue potential donors. Kathy and Tina said they would be in touch regarding the testing and we chatted awhile longer. As they were leaving, I thought how sweet and positive-minded the two of them were, which amazed me considering their constant exposure to all of this sickness and death.

Several months later Pat confessed that he had been nervous about having to give the blood because he thought he would be jabbed with a needle for each of the eight vials required. He didn't realize that they inserted just one needle and then attached the refill vials to it. Like me, he had never been seriously ill and had rarely had the need to go to a doctor. We were both very naïve about illness and the medical system. I should add, fondly, that I knew he was a big chicken about needles and this made me appreciate all the more what he was volunteering to do for me.

Lying in bed, my thoughts returned to the reading material I had been given and the section on how the matching was done for a donor. I had learned that the matching is a very complicated process. To understand the matching one must understand bone marrow. Bone marrow is made up of stem cells that are the source of blood production and the body's immune system which involves leukocytes or in layman's terms, white cells. Leukocytes play a major role in the immune system. Modern technology makes it possible to identify an individual's precise DNA sequence of Human Leukocyte Antigen (HLA) genes (alleles). This is the crux of finding a match. Preferably five HLA alleles must match between donor and recipient for a doable transplant. A matching of six alleles was coveted. You would think that this would have been easier to understand considering all of the "House" episodes I had watched, but it was not. Surprisingly, it did not matter if you and the donor were of the same blood type although it was a bonus. What was critical was the matching of the alleles. There was a number relating to the match that indicated how good a match it was. For instance, a full sibling match (not a twin) was considered a "6" indicating the sixth allele was matched. The number could not be less than four because your chances of the transplant working or "engrafting" into your bone marrow were small and if you did engraft, the complications could be fatal. Identical twins had it "made" because their twin sibling was an exact duplicate of their own DNA. The only caveat to that would be identifying whether the donating twin had the same disease as the recipient. Needless to say, no transplant would be done given that scenario. To fully understand the complexity of finding a match, a recent national paper contained an excellent article on the subject. It stated that if everyone in the entire world had their bone marrow tested and identified, or "typed" as it is commonly referred to, there would still be recipients with no match. Such were the odds that I was faced with.

I started thinking about Pat…my only real hope at that point. Pat was 18 months older than I. As children, we fought like cats and dogs, partly a result I feel of both parents working and too much time spent alone without supervision. Our relationship as adults was civil, but our lives and marriages took us in different directions. After Bob and I got together, we moved several times and always far away. The geographical distance, as well as dissimilar interests, created an emotional detachment between Pat and me. Our reunions were infrequent but we did speak on the phone regularly. What we did know was that we loved each other and should one need the other, we would be there in a blink. I think the "blink" had arrived! My mother told me later that Pat couldn't run to the laboratory fast enough to be tested. He was very worried that he would not be a match and I found out from other sibling donors that the guilt is awful if they do not. To know that you could save your brother or sister's life and then to not be able to, had to be a terrible burden to bear even though the outcome was beyond your control. A powerful bond began to develop between Pat and me. Through adversity, we had now come together as adults and I would soon realize how similar we actually were.

Later in the afternoon, Gavin came in to tell me that I would be receiving my first platelet transfusion the following day. The results from that morning's blood tests revealed that I had reached the critical stage and needed "topping up." I learned that when people donate blood, the blood can be "sifted" to isolate the platelets and then, they alone can be given to patients. Each platelet transfusion was enough to last about five days depending on the individual. Gavin then said that after my transfusion, I would be discharged if my condition continued to be stable. Apparently, some people can have very serious reactions to blood product transfusions and they would see how I handled my first one. At that point, other than being terribly weak, having no breath, and only mouth sores to deal with, I wasn't considered at risk to leave the hospital. I was sort of "healthy."

In a way, I was afraid to leave because I felt very vulnerable. I voiced this concern to Gavin and he said he had been planning to give me a list of things not to do while at home. First of all, I was not to go grocery shopping unless it was at times when there were virtually no people in the store and if I did choose to go, I was to wear a mask. Silently I laughed at that idea; I couldn't even get out of bed let alone head to the grocery store. Great...I could just picture myself walking into a supermarket wearing a mask. They'd probably call in the police fearing that they were about to be robbed. Talk about drawing attention to yourself. Also, I was not to go in our barn or be near our horses. Apparently, breathing in mold from hay or bacteria from manure could give me a deadly lung infection or, worse yet, a fungal brain infection that could permanently affect my memory or even kill me. I met a patient a few months later that had suffered from such an infection, and he could no longer find his way to a bathroom he had been to countless times. Going home was sounding less and less like a good idea with each passing second. I mentioned to Gavin that I had dozens of plants and he said not to go near those for the same reasons relating to the fungus and mold threat. All right, so now I couldn't be near people, I couldn't go in the barn, couldn't be near the horses, couldn't be near my plants…what the hell could I be near? Oh yes, Bob… provided he remained healthy.

Well, before I could even ask, Gavin said that if I had any pets, I shouldn't be near them either. I told him that was impossible but I did promise him that I would keep them off the bed and I wouldn't pet them. Our doggies were not going to be pleased about this change to their lifestyle. I thought we had covered everything but there was, of course, more. Somehow I was not surprised…there was no end to the "DON'T" list. Gavin knew that my mouth sores were getting worse so he suggested that I stop using a toothbrush and start using a special little gizmo that was a sort of wooden stick resembling a tongue depressor with a small piece of square sponge glued to the tip. Well, the idea was to gently "brush" your teeth so that you did not tear your gums or the insides of your mouth. Firstly, if you did rip your gums open, it would put you at risk for yet more infections and secondly, any abrasions to the gums would cause bleeding because of my low platelet count. Later on I developed my own "toothbrush" which was a simple Q-tip that was easier to manipulate over my teeth and gave a better sense of clean than the wooden stick. As I had mentioned before, because your mouth is filled with bacteria, there is great emphasis on oral hygiene. I knew of patients who had died as a result of complications stemming from a mouth infection. A movie scenario came to mind; I think I must have watched too much TV as a child. I thought about this futuristic 1982 Arnold Schwarzenegger movie called *"The Running Man"* where Arnold was pitted against all sorts of dangers and his mission was to see if he could survive them. If he survived, the prize was that his life would be spared. I had become Arnold.

I thought we had covered everything, but Gavin had one more thing to say. He mentioned that I could not receive any flowers from well-wishers because of yet again, the mold and fungus issue. Hearing this saddened me since one of my greatest passions had always been flowers. So that put the kibosh on just about everything that gave me pleasure other than music. At least, my ears were not at risk...not yet anyway...I was afraid to ask. Gavin finished and said that if there was anything else I needed to know to just buzz the nurses' station. I could not imagine what else there could be for me to ask – my entire life had been turned upside down!

Later in the afternoon, Bob returned and I passed on everything that happened while he had been at home. He was pleased to hear that things were progressing in terms of Pat being tested and was even more pleased to hear that they were planning on discharging me the following day. His euphoria at the news of my leaving the hospital though was short lived as he listened to each "DON'T" as advised by Gavin. When I told him that I would be receiving my first platelet transfusion, Bob's face became even wearier. I think if we could have, we would have run away together to parts unknown.

As per our usual routine of two nights, Bob had brought the little cooler with his libation. He poured his chardonnay into a plastic cup...our surroundings were a stark contrast to our normal cocktail hour at home in our family room with the fireplace lit or sitting on our front porch watching horses peacefully grazing. We sat there for a while and talked about what was new at our farm. That seemed like such a faraway place to me and it felt as if I had not been there in years. I was dying (a bad choice of words, perhaps) to see the dogs, yet at the same time I was afraid to go home with all of the dangers that it held for me. I did not voice this to Bob because I didn't want him to take it personally but I knew he had to feel much the same. Who wouldn't…I'd be terrified to have the responsibility of having to look after someone like me! The evening continued with Bob getting his regular pizza and me getting something that resembled food. Eating was becoming a real "pain in the gums" and even with the numbing powers of the "Swish and Spit," my heart just wasn't in it. I forced most of it down…I had to.

Wednesday morning came with the usual 5:30 a.m. poke and blood-letting. After the nurse left, we stayed in bed for another hour desperately trying to catch 40 winks to make up for yet another sleepless night. Bob packed up his cot and looked forward to our being at home that evening and in our own bed. Before he left, Bob had to give me a sponge bath because I had become so feeble that I was no longer able to stand and shower. It was such a sweet thing to do and for as long as I live, I will never forget the tenderness and sadness with which he did it. I think he felt that this was one of the few things he could do for me because everything else seemed to be out of his power.

I thought about Bob after he left and how he was coping with all of this. We did have highly competent people that worked for us but because we had such a huge property and complicated lifestyle with the horses and dogs, not to mention our retail business, it was still a lot on one person's plate. I knew what my day was like when I was healthy and at home… I never stopped for one second. I could only imagine what Bob was going through having to do so much more and be the liaison between myself and everyone who wanted updates as to my status. As Maggie had said to me the day before, the caregiver was in so many cases the unsung hero. I was realizing more and more what she had meant by that.

The remaining part of the morning was routine which meant that the nurses came in regularly to do their vitals check and the resident hematologist stopped by to examine me. Every two hours a nurse would take my temperature to ensure that it was still normal…fevers had to be caught early or avoided altogether if at all possible. I had been told by Gavin that during my stay at home, we should monitor my temperature regularly and should it go higher than 100.2°F, we were to head to the emergency room at McMaster University Hospital immediately. I had also been told to watch for urinary tract infections as that could become a bigger problem. It seemed that every part of my body could turn against me. With each danger that I was told about, my thoughts returned to what it had been like to be healthy. That seemed a distant memory. How I wished I had appreciated my health more but generally, and sadly so, one doesn't think about something until it is gone. I now know that the most important thing in life is to have good health...without it, you have nothing

In the afternoon, Gavin came by to tell me that my platelets would be arriving shortly and that barring any problems I would be discharged by 3:30 p.m. or so. This whole transfusion thing made me very nervous. I had no idea what to expect or how it was going to feel. At about 3:00 p.m., the platelets still had not arrived and Gavin came in to say there was a mix-up in the blood type and they had received the wrong platelets. Why couldn't at least one thing go according to plan I thought? A new order had been placed at the blood bank and it would not reach the hospital for another hour or so. Obviously, a 3:30 p.m. discharge was not going to happen. When Bob arrived, he had expected to see me ready to go and was very disappointed that the transfusion wasn't even underway yet. As the minutes ticked by and we waited for the platelets, my feeling of impatience turned to one of anxiety. What if there were no platelets of my somewhat rare blood type, B Negative? What if my platelets did not arrive at all? My mind raced into paranoiac overdrive.

Eventually around 4:30 p.m., Gavin and another nurse arrived with the platelet bag. Relief washed over me. I vowed never to be impatient again when it came to waiting for blood products. My new philosophy was to be thankful that someone had donated their blood that enabled me to live another day. The time had come for my first transfusion. There is a formal protocol for such things in that two nurses are involved in the start of the procedure. Gavin read the name on my hospital ID wristband and the other nurse read the tag attached to the platelet bag. I thought this rather strange at first wondering why he would read my name on my wristband since he knew who I was. The reason for this I learned was that there would be no error made in a patient receiving the wrong transfusion. Wristband and blood product tag had to match and it had to be read by two people so that no overworked or overtired nurse could make an error. Once everything was verified, the other nurse departed leaving Gavin to insert the IV into my arm. He asked me to let him know if I started to feel ill and then said that if everything went well, the transfusion would take about 45 minutes. After about a quarter of an hour and feeling satisfied that I was not having any reactions, Gavin left. He would check in at intervals to make sure that I was not having any problems.

I was fairly nervous and hadn't really wanted to look at the "stuff" in this bag but my curiosity got the better of me. I was surprised to see that platelets were whitish pink in color and quite thick in texture. No wonder their role was to clot your blood: they even looked pasty. Bob watched me as I sat there and I knew that he felt as strange about this as I did. As the contents of the bag lessened, I exhibited no side effects. Gavin came back before the bag was finished and then watched while it emptied to the last drop. Waste not want not certainly applied here. He asked me how I felt and I said that other than a couple of tickly spots on my arm and back, I was fine. I then learned the itchy areas were a reaction to the platelets, namely hives and I was disappointed to be told that I would have to stay in the hospital for yet another hour so that Gavin could monitor me. Nothing was left to chance! Even though I ended up with only two hives, future transfusions would have to be preceded by a dose of Benadryl to avoid any increase in allergic reaction. We waited the hour and with no further complications, I was given the all clear to go home.

Just prior to our leaving, Gavin gave me a card with an appointment time for the following Monday. From now until my transplant, assuming a match was found, I would have to go to the outpatient clinic in the ward every few days so that my blood levels could be evaluated. I would have to go for blood tests prior to the appointment, and then once the results were in the doctors would decide if I needed any hemoglobin or platelet transfusions. If everything stayed stable, that would be my life for the next few weeks. In essence, I would be kept alive by transfusions. You may wonder why one was not given white cell or leukocyte transfusions…the reason is that a white cell has only a life span of several hours and it is not logical to transfuse them. I was also given a box of hospital masks and instructed to put one on when I came back for my appointments. That would lessen my chances of catching something – as if aplastic anemia wasn't enough!

Having covered all of the bases, we were ready to go and considering how weak I felt, Bob got me a wheelchair. We went downstairs and I had to wait in the lobby while Bob brought the car around to the front entrance of the hospital. I must have seemed a sad soul sitting there by myself, mask on and lifeless.

Once Bob arrived, he helped me out of the wheelchair and into our car. After about five minutes in the car, I started to tremble uncontrollably. I was absolutely frozen and my teeth began chattering like one of those prank set of dentures. I think it was a reaction to the platelets coupled with the psychological shock of my first transfusion. By the time we got home, things had not improved and consequently Bob put me in bed and heaped several blankets on me. After what seemed like an eternity, I gradually began to warm up and the shaking stopped. Our dogs had displayed such joy at seeing me and I had barely been able to give them a second look. I knew they would forgive me; our dogs were such kind souls.

Now we were on our own…Bob, me, and my disease. It was an unsettling feeling but we knew that in five days we would be back in the hospital for my outpatient appointment. If only I could stay "well" until then. When Bob was satisfied that I was comfortable, he announced that he would make me something for dinner. Our master bedroom was only steps from the kitchen and while Bob was preparing my meal I could offer instructions if he needed to know where something was or what to do. On several occasions he had to come back to the bedroom because he could not hear my frail voice. I never thought I would see the day where I would be completely helpless, and Bob would be doing the cooking. Life is strange sometimes.

When Bob brought in my dinner, there was pride in his eyes. He never cooked and I appreciated what a massive effort it was for him given he wasn't a natural in the kitchen. Sitting on the tray were a grilled cheese sandwich cut in triangular fashion and a bowl of lukewarm tomato soup. Gone were the days of eating anything piping hot…the condition of my mouth could not have handled that. Honestly, Bob could have fed me the worst meal on this earth and I would have eaten it…not because I was hungry, but because he had prepared it with such love. It took me awhile but with the aid of the "Swish and Spit" I was able to finish off most of what I had been served. Bob was pleased with my determination to eat. He knew it wasn't easy for me.

During my supper, our Brittany, Dudley, kept trying to jump up on the bed and repeatedly Bob had to tell him to get off. Dudley couldn't understand why all of a sudden this was verboten territory. By evening's end, Dudley had adjusted to the new rules and resigned himself to staying on the floor. Thankfully, our 90-lb. Shepherd, Max, had never had any inclination to be a "bed dog." He was your typical, loyal German Shepherd especially towards Bob. We could have lived in a hovel with barely a scrap to eat and Max would have been happy as long as we were with him. Once Bob cleaned up from dinner we visited awhile longer in the bedroom. By this time, I was exhausted and hoped that I would be able to sleep. Bob, needing some "down time," settled into our family room and watched sports on TV. It was a welcome, mindless diversion for him.

Chapter 4
September 8th to September 10th

The ensuing few days followed the same routine. Bob would get up in the mornings and perform all of the tasks which had been mine. The dogs were let out and then fed. Next on the list was making coffee and emptying the dishwasher followed by a general tidying up of the kitchen. All of this was done while I was stuck in that forsaken bed. Becoming quite adept at breakfast, Bob scrambled some eggs, made toast and cut up various fruits which he placed in a decorative fashion on the plate. I guess he had noticed all my small touches over all those years. I made every effort to eat what he had so lovingly prepared for me. Once breakfast was done, he began his usual array of outside jobs. Normally this would have included the daily riding and training of our horses, but this had to be put on the back burner. Neither of us would be riding at this point – me for obvious reasons and Bob because he was much too busy. Thankfully, we had barn staff who kept up with the daily stall cleaning, feeding and basic looking after of the horses. What could not be put off however, were any farm repairs that had to be done of which there were always a steady stream and property maintenance such as mowing and trimming of our 24-acre property. All of this only added to the stress level of what we were going through…Bob because he had to keep up with it all and me because I couldn't offer a scrap of help. Mike took time away from his managerial responsibilities at our retail business in order to help Bob with the mowing and gardening.

This was extremely appreciated by both of us.

During his chores, Bob would stop in regularly to check on me and take my temperature. By mid-afternoon of my first full day home, much to our dismay, my temperature was slowly on the rise. We were hoping that I would not reach the magic number of 100.2°F before Monday because that meant of course, that I would have to head back to emergency at McMaster and be admitted again. It was apparent that my body was fighting some kind of an underlying infection that had not yet fully revealed itself. Bob continued to check on me frequently and brought me whatever I needed. While I was glued to the bed, and trust me, that was what it felt like, I would see him running past our bedroom doorway working on one thing or another. I thought back to the scene in the Wizard of Oz where the Wicked Witch of the West melted into the floor and I envisioned that soon all that would be left of me was a pair of crumpled pajamas lying atop the sheets. I felt totally useless and guilty!

Since I could not move around, I did use this time to make some phone calls. At least that was one thing I was still able to do, provided I didn't run out of oxygen too quickly. I soon learned that I could only speak a couple of sentences at a time and then had to take a break before I could continue. It was as if I had done the 1000 yard dash and couldn't speak from the exhaustion. My mother nearly began to cry when she heard the difficulty I was having. I'm sure she could not conceive that this frail voice belonged to her daughter who had always been incredibly active and the epitome of good health. The sadness and distress in her voice was heartbreaking and only re-confirmed how truly ill I must have sounded. Thank goodness my aunt was there to help her through this ordeal. After I hung up, I called Pat and Linda. Pat had just had his blood work done the day before and was already impatiently awaiting the results. I cannot imagine what it would feel like knowing that you are holding someone else's life in your hands. As we chatted, he was full of confidence saying that he had no doubts that he would be a match. I had difficulty in subscribing to the same optimism knowing what I had read regarding the odds of finding a match. We continued to talk with Pat filling in when I had to rest. If he was disturbed by my inconsistent speech patterns, he gave no indication of it. I love him for many reasons but especially for his never ending outward support during my illness. Perhaps behind closed doors he was less so but I will never know. I promised to call him nightly after he got home from work.

In the evenings, Bob continued to serve up dinner in our bedroom. I had my bed tray and Bob set up a TV tray next to the bed for himself. What a surreal scene it must have been. Here we were cognizant of the incredible odds facing us and our dogs slept peacefully on the floor as if nothing in the world was wrong. I again wished I were a dog. After Bob tidied up, we played Scrabble. We had always loved the game and it was the perfect distraction since it required total concentration. We welcomed a break from our worries even if I could only last a couple of games.

During those few days, when I did have an occasional 15-minute burst of energy, I would try and email friends or write instructions for Bob pertaining to our bookkeeping. There was no way I was leaving this earth without being organized! Needless to say, most of my time in bed was spent thinking and thinking. When I wasn't thinking about Bob being left alone in the event that I died, I was thinking about whether Pat would be a match. Our doctor friend Janet had suggested I begin developing positive thinking techniques to help me through the difficult times that lay ahead. She obviously knew more about what I was to face than I did. I decided to scan and print an old school photograph of Pat and me that was taken when we were 6 and 4^1/$_2$ years old, respectively. For the occasion, my mother

Pat and Esther, aged 6 and 4 1/2

had dressed us in matching outfits and we actually looked very twin-like. I posted it on the mirror across from our bed. I would look at that photo for hours on end, listening to music and thinking to myself… "You have to match, we are twins, you have to match, we are twins." Many times I was disheartened thinking of the minute chance that Pat would actually be a match, but then I would just start my chant again pushing it from my mind. I'm sure that Bob thought I was crazy, but at that point he figured anything was worth a try.

A few friends dropped by during those four days and they were all incredulous as to what we were faced with. They should have been in this body! Many of them offered to be tested as a possible donor match but, realistically, the probability of that happening was basically nil. When they came to visit, they had to sit about six feet away from me and I couldn't hug or kiss them in case they had anything contagious. The whole thing was bizarre. Some brought flowers which painfully had to be placed outside on our front porch. My old friend Bev from Texas wired me a beautiful floral arrangement and I never had the heart to tell her that I couldn't even bring it in the house. Overall, we discouraged visitations from anyone because we just couldn't risk any contamination.

My body was starting to cry "Uncle" to the lack of a functioning immune system. Suddenly, I developed hemorrhoids that would have given George Brett (a baseball player in the early 80's who was sidelined because of severe hemorrhoids) a run for his money. In addition, I got a bladder infection which I had never had in my life. My mouth continued to deteriorate and I could not even use the wooden makeshift toothbrush with the sponge because any "brushing" would cause my gums to start bleeding. This was when I decided to use the Q-tip as my toothbrush…as they say, necessity is the mother of invention!

Each time something new would crop up, we phoned the hospital and they would give us a prescription or advice that would help us deal with the latest physical crisis. What would be considered normal health issues for most people became terrifying to us because everything could lead to a more serious secondary infection or uncontrolled bleeding. I was constantly watching for more bruising because that would mean that I was hemorrhaging. The original bruises on my arms still looked terrible and I noticed that where my veins had normally bulged outwards, there were now sagging depressions! I felt as if I was drying up due to lack of blood. It got to the point where it actually made me sick to look at myself because it only reminded me of how ill I was.

It seemed so ludicrous to me now that I had actually worried about getting older and getting wrinkles and sagging skin. I had bought every new cream product on the market in an effort to outsmart Mother Nature. Maybe that gave me aplastic anemia…only kidding, wouldn't that have been ironic? Now I laugh when I see skin product commercials with young women worrying about their non-existent facial wrinkles. "Get a life!" I think. What I would give to be healthy AND WRINKLED! I vowed, if I lived, never to worry about getting old again. (One does much "vowing" when faced with death.) Hell, I would just be happy to get old. A birthday card came to mind that I had given Bob and truer words were never written…"The more birthdays you have, the longer you live." At this point, it looked like I wasn't even going to make it to my 50th birthday. How I had taken for granted that I would turn 50. A few months prior I had joked with Bob about the type of party I would like to have when I turned a half-century. Why does one always assume that tomorrow or next year will be there? It was a shame that aplastic anemia had to be my wake-up call to life and what was truly important.

Those five days felt like an eternity because we were living on pins and needles in terms of my declining condition. Bob kept checking my temperature and by Sunday, I wasn't far off the 100.2°F mark. In an effort to reduce my fever, Bob got a basin of cold water and sponged me down repeatedly. Frankly, I didn't think much of that because with each application of the cold water I would shake like a leaf but I knew it had to be done. Bob was able to bring down my temperature by a couple of degrees. That would bide us enough time until the following day which was Monday, and my first appointment as an outpatient.

That evening, I was so stressed that I could barely eat. Bob was disappointed but did not press the issue. We didn't play Scrabble – our minds couldn't concentrate on that. There was an incredible incident that occurred that night. Part of Bob's nightly routine during the years of our horse ownership was to head to the barn between 9:00 p.m. and 10:00 p.m. to perform a "night check" of our horses. This simply meant that he would do a visual on each horse by giving them a piece of carrot and their response would tell him if any one of them was not well. Most horse owners did this. Many people think horses are invincible, but those in the know, understand that they are extremely fragile animals. That particular evening, Bob walked into the barn and proceeded to give all of the horses a carrot as per usual. As he entered the stall of a gelding named CC, the horse walked up to Bob and began to sniff his neck. CC's nostrils flared wide open and it was as if he was inhaling Bob's skin. He continued this for five minutes. CC and I had always had a special relationship because he was an abused ex-race horse and I had been working with him for almost two years. When Bob came back to the house, he told me about CC's behavior. We suddenly realized that before Bob had headed to the barn he had come in to give me a hug and I had snuggled into his neck. Using a horse's incredible sense of smell, CC had recognized my scent on Bob's skin. I felt saddened that I couldn't see him but it warmed my heart to know that the hundreds of hours of painstaking training had not been for naught…he had remembered me.

Chapter 5

September 11ᵗʰ to September 13ᵗʰ

In the morning, Bob thought I should pack a few things for the hospital in the event something went wrong and they needed to admit me again. He must have been clairvoyant on that one. As I was finishing blow drying my hair, I almost fainted and had to sit down on the edge of the bed. I was incredibly dizzy and it took me a while before I could get up again. It seemed that even the simple task of blow drying my hair was too much of an exertion for me. I could not fathom why I felt this way and mentioned it to Bob. We couldn't drive to the hospital fast enough. We were both tired of dealing with all of these unexpected and unexplained health issues that plagued me without ever a moment's relief.

When we arrived at the hospital, I put my mask on and Bob got me a wheelchair and took me to the lab to have my blood taken. I felt like such an invalid and I could see people staring at me and strangely enough, I didn't give two hoots! I was beyond the point of caring what people thought. The lab was a "take a number" system. When my number was called, I had been told to inform the technician that I was a patient of Dr. Wasi's and that they would have my name on a list created daily by Ward 3Z. Indeed they did, and we entered a room where my blood was taken. Obviously, these people were trained to be very careful in situations such as these and they put gloves on to take my blood so that they didn't pass on any undesirables. Truth be told, they were just as concerned about their own safety and health and what a patient could pass on to them. After I "donated," they gave us a baggie with my blood vials and gave us directions to the processing laboratory in the hospital. For the rank and file walking into the clinic and having their blood taken, a volunteer would take the tubes down to the lab. Once you were a regular patient and on THE LIST, you knew it was faster to take the blood down yourself rather than wait to have it taken down.

After we dropped off my blood, Bob wheeled me to the blood disorder ward waiting room. It was a long narrow room with mismatched chairs lining both sides. Two people sat at a table at the far end playing euchre. In a corner adjacent to the table, stood an old, rickety cabinet filled with used, tattered books. I couldn't accuse the ward of wasting valuable funds on décor. None of these rooms did much to raise anyone's spirits. (The ward has since moved to a new, modern location with upbeat décor for patients and staff alike.) Bob pushed me to the end of the room since nearly every chair was taken and found us a space close to the table where there was a vacant chair. Satisfied that I was comfortable, Bob then headed to the registration desk. While he was gone, I looked around and noted the general demeanor of everyone in attendance. This was not a happy group, which came as no surprise. It occurred to me that I was not the only one in this "boat." Laughter suddenly erupted from the table and I took note of the young woman and older gentleman sitting there. They were teasing each other unmercifully. It was a welcome diversion to watch them. I marveled at their sense of humor given the morose atmosphere in the room. When Bob returned, he said that our name would be called over the intercom when they were ready to see us. While we waited, we learned that the couple playing euchre was in fact father and daughter. The man was in his early seventies and the woman I guessed to be in her early forties. Later that day, we saw them again in the outpatient room and learned that he was terminally ill with leukemia. That was our first real exposure to the tenuousness of life as a patient in Ward 3Z.

For over an hour we sat and waited. We took this opportunity to make up a detailed list of the things that we wanted to ask Dr. Wasi when we saw her. We had been told the week before that these were typically long days and to bring a lunch and be prepared to stay well into the afternoon. Our appointment was for 10:30 a.m. and in our ignorance, we actually thought that we would be on our way by about 1:00 p.m. We soon learned why the "wait" was in "waiting room." Shortly after 11:30 a.m. our name was called and we were instructed to go into the "Day-Care" clinic room where outpatients were given their transfusions, chemotherapy or any other medications via IV or permanent catheter.

Let me tell you…that was one somber sight! The room contained about 20 large, vinyl-cushioned chairs and a few small beds. Most of the chairs were pea green or faded orange and showed extreme use. Each chair or bed was occupied by a person hooked up to tubing that led to a bag hanging from a metal pole that moved by way of castors. Several nurses were in attendance and they were scurrying about from one patient to the next….sort of like a pit crew in action. Despite the depressing sight, the nurses were joking and carrying on with different patients. As I said before, these people were optimistic most of the time. One of them wheeled me to a corner and checked my blood pressure and the level of oxygen in my blood. The oxygen was checked by putting a metal clothespin looking affair on the end of my finger which was hooked up to a sensor and it indicated that levels were normal. I had no idea what that meant. Then the nurse pulled my face mask down to insert the thermometer into my mouth to take my temperature. She laughed in pleasant surprise at the fact that I had actually put rouge and lipstick on. I guess in retrospect it was strange; I'm sure most women feeling the way I did wouldn't bother putting any make-up on. For me, it was something that I had always done and it didn't matter to me that I was literally standing at death's door. My mother's favorite expression came to mind, "If you look good, you feel good!" Well, it's not that I felt good but I would have felt worse had I not had my face on. The nurse commented that my temperature was fine no doubt due to the cold sponging from the night before. Thank goodness for that.

Shortly afterwards, I was informed that the lab results had come in and that I was going to need a blood transfusion…two bags worth! That answered the question as to why I had nearly passed out that morning. My hemoglobin count was 78 and the low normal for women is *115*. I had been running on fumes. I just kept hoping that when the blood arrived and started flowing that I wouldn't pass out at the sight of it. Bob took the opportunity to ask one of the nurses when we would be seeing the doctor and she said that we would be there for quite a while so not to worry – we would see her eventually. We learned that a blood transfusion takes about 2-3 hours per bag because it has to flow at the same rate as your own blood pressure otherwise there is chance of blowing an artery. Nothing was simple.

After about an hour, a volunteer brought a fabric shopping bag which was filled with numerous blood and platelet bags for various patients. One of the nurses brought a pole over and hung my bag of blood on it. They then verified that it was indeed the blood meant for me and started the machine which controlled the flow. Surprisingly I didn't pass out at the sight of it. I guess when you know that something will save your life you stare it in the face and get over your fears. The transfusion itself seemed to take forever with the time dragging on endlessly. We kept looking up each time a white-coated person walked in anticipating the arrival of my hematologist, Dr. Wasi. Repeatedly we were disappointed. I dared take a quick glance around at the other patients because I didn't want to seem as if I was staring. Most people were absorbed in their own little world spending the time either reading or listening to an iPod. The odd one was sleeping which brought a no doubt welcome, albeit momentary feeling of oblivion to their current problems. Very few spoke to one another and if they did, I had the impression that there was a connection between them as if they were members of a secret society. What we found very strange was that when a doctor did come in, they spoke to their patient in front of everyone. There seemed to be no concern for that patient's privacy or that other people would overhear what was going on. What I learned afterwards was that at that point you were so ill that you did not care if anyone overheard, and you were just relieved that a doctor had finally come in to speak with you.

Finally, around 3:30 p.m., the young intern who had done the aspiration during my stay in the hospital came in to see us. Bob had my list of things to ask and began with our questions. Most of the items on the list related to such things as my bruising, sore and bleeding gums, bladder infections, hemorrhoids, etc. One thing we had not talked about with anyone was our concern over my getting a menstrual period. Because I had started perimenopause, my monthly cycles had become erratic and I had not had a period since May of that year and now we were in September but, as all women know, it did not mean I was finished with the whole "business." Knowing the luck I seemed to be having, we feared that it would show up while my platelets were in the tank. Our worry was that if I did get a period, how would it be stopped? The intern looked at us as if we were boring her with incidental queries and did not seem too concerned saying that we would deal with that if and when the problem arose. This did not really comfort me a great deal and I remember thinking that if the shoe were on the other foot, I don't think lady you'd be taking this as casually. I have always been the kind of person to have a plan A, B and C along with five contingencies just in case, and this type of noncommittal answer did not fill me with confidence! Nonetheless, we did not say anything else and just hoped that Murphy's Law would not come into play. How lucky we are that we cannot predict the future. At this point, Bob asked her if he could speak to her in private outside of the Day Care room and she reluctantly followed him. I think she knew she would be asked questions that required difficult answers and I don't think she had the experience or personality to deal with anyone's emotions. No wonder she was dragging her feet on the way out.

Bob had told me he wanted to inquire how things were progressing with the typing of Pat's blood and how much longer that was going to take, but his real reason was that he wanted to ask her what my chances were of surviving the transplant given my current condition and age. When he asked her the question, no doubt the one she hoped he would not ask, the resident replied that even with a match my chances of survival were 30%. If you looked at it another way, I had a 70% chance of dying. Bob never mentioned this part of the conversation to me at the time and it was no wonder he looked terribly distressed when he came back into the room. Sometimes it's best to be kept in the dark.

By the time Bob came back in, my transfusion was finished and one of the nurses unhooked me and as part of procedure took my temperature again. She took a double take at the monitor when she read that my temperature had leapt to over 102°F! I had felt extremely tired and chilly during the afternoon, but had attributed it to the stress of being in this environment for the first time. No doubt whatever my underlying infection was, it had surfaced again along with some reaction to the blood transfusion. Some people react to blood transfusions and I guess I was one of those not so lucky ones.

She quickly called the intern in and upon reading my chart we were advised that I was not leaving the hospital. Bob and I looked at each other in desperation, feeling that we were descending deeper and deeper into a giant sinkhole. Were we ever going to get a break? It seemed not. The nurse wheeled me into a private room followed by Bob and the resident at which point she performed a more detailed examination and re-confirmed that with such a high fever, I would not be leaving. The overnight bag that Bob had suggested I bring would be put to good use after all.

I naturally assumed that I would be going back into the 3Z Ward and the look on my face must have been one of utter disbelief at the news that there were no beds available and that I would have to wait it out in the emergency room until a bed opened up for me. To make matters worse, the nurse added that I could possibly even be there until the wee hours of the morning. Bob and I were speechless hearing this because even though we were new to this world, we knew that with the fever I was even more vulnerable than normal, and we couldn't fathom the logic of placing me in an area filled with bacteria and sick people! I could see that Bob was reaching the boiling point and he said with admirable self-control that he did not think this was a good idea. They answered that there was no choice…there was simply no room.

It was decided that they would start me on a bag of antibiotics pronto to get the fever under control. After hooking up the bag to the pole and the pole to the chair, my nurse wheeled me to the emergency room with Bob following closely behind. Once we got there, the nurse did explain my condition and my neutropenic status (no immune function) to the triage staff and she requested that I be kept in a private examination room until such time as a bed opened up. This did little to console us. Once in the room, Bob helped me to the bed and positioned the pole so that the tubing would not be strained. We looked at each other completely shell-shocked and felt like passengers on a continuous downhill roller coaster ride…destination…hell.

We had been there since 8:00 a.m. and now it was approaching 5:30 p.m. This turn of events had not been part of our agenda and even though Bob had arranged for our barn employee to feed the dogs and let them out, there were no plans for someone to stay overnight at our house. This meant that Bob would have to go home and leave me until he could come back the following morning. It was the last thing he wanted to do, but he had no choice. Before Bob left, he found me some bottled water and while doing so, asked one of the emergency nurses to keep an eye on me. He was very worried, as was I, that I would be forgotten due to the main focus being on incoming triage patients and not on a woman left in an isolated room who didn't even belong there. Bob and I hugged and reluctantly he headed for home. The door closed with an ominous, vault-like sound.

With difficulty, I sat up in bed and looked around my dungeon (for that was how it felt). The room was cement block in that shade of bluish green that seemed to be standard hospital issue. Other than my bed, a couple of chairs and a metal cart topped with medical supplies, the room was bare. The bleakness of the room mirrored my outlook. For the past 12 days, tortuous bit by tortuous bit, my health had been taken away from me and were it not for the kind souls that donated blood products I probably would have been six feet under already. How much longer could I be kept alive and what awful illness would I eventually succumb to? I had seen the resigned looks and emaciated bodies of some of the patients in Ward 3Z awaiting their inevitable final outcome. The absolute desperation I felt was unimaginable. Things just kept getting worse and if you thought they couldn't get any worse, lo and behold, they did. I wished that I could cry because I felt that somehow it would make me feel better, but, despite everything, I could produce no tears. I lay on the bed and thought about my life and where it was going, or not going! This was the first time that I started to feel that living wasn't worth what I was going through. The non-stop daily torment of my own body waging war on me and the constant fear that came with it, began to take its toll on me psychologically. I now understood how people could just give up on life…I began to view dying as a welcome escape. I knew from the reading material that my odds were not good to survive a transplant, let alone the fact that I didn't even know if I had a match. I had to have some hope and right now, I believed that there was none.

Mother Nature intervened my dark thinking and I realized that my bladder was telling me I could no longer put off going to the bathroom. There was only one option and it meant taking my pole and heading OUT THERE into the main area of the emergency room where all of the patients sat with their accompanying family or friends. As much as I hated this cell and wanted out, I imagined everyone on the outside not as people but as giant microbes with human heads. Mask on, I grabbed my pole and slowly opened the door looking one way and then the other noting that my destination was just a few short steps directly across from my room. Holding my breath and walking as quickly as possible, I entered the bathroom, exhaling deeply while closing the door. The procedure of doing what I had to do and remaining uninfected by the invisible threats would have made Howard Hughes proud. I was beginning to understand how an obsession with hygiene could take hold of an individual. Grasping the door handle with my shirt, I exited and made my way back.

Two hours passed, during which time not a single soul came in to check on me…they were too busy dealing with car accident victims, bar brawl injuries and the like. I could have gone into cardiac arrest and no one would have been the wiser. Finally, there was a knock on the door and an orderly entered pushing a gurney. I couldn't have been more thrilled…I was being saved from this awful place and from my own morbid thoughts. The orderly told me a bed had been found, not in 3Z, but in another ward that dealt with more common illnesses. I didn't care where I was being sent, as long as I got out of this hell hole!

By the time I got wheeled to the new ward which happened to be on the same floor as 3Z, it was about 10:30 p.m. I was barely in the room and transferred to the bed when my knight in shining armor appeared…BOB! If I hadn't already been lying down, I would have keeled over at the wonderful shock of seeing him suddenly arrive. This was completely unexpected. Bob told me he had driven home breaking all land and speed records and had planned, that if stopped by a policeman, to tell him the whole saga fully expecting to be released without a ticket and perhaps even being escorted back to the hospital. Once home, he called Mike and organized for him to stay the night with our dogs and then had thrown some toiletries and a change of clothes into a carry-on bag. Bob had taken a few minutes to call Janet and discuss my unscheduled temporary "confinement" in emergency hoping that she would offer some advice or guidance. We will never know to this day whether it was Janet's influence or just good fortune that freed up a bed for me, but the bottom line was that by the time Bob returned to the hospital I had one and we were not asking any questions as to how or why.

Shortly after Bob came in, a nurse arrived to get our personal information although by the empathetic, sad look in her eyes, I could tell that she had already been advised of some of my background. As with all the other nurses that I had met so far, she was caring, attentive and sensitive. Once the forms were out of the way, she left saying that a cot would be found for Bob and if we needed anything, to press the buzzer. This room was a bit larger than the one in 3Z but the downside was that the bathroom was not a private one and had to be shared with a woman in the adjoining room. I decided beggars couldn't be choosers.

After such a traumatic day, Bob and I were beyond exhaustion and welcomed the arrival of the cot and sheets. Knowing the routine now, Bob set it up complete with bedding in no time at all and we promptly settled into our beds for some much needed sleep. It was not to be had. By midnight, we hadn't slept a wink and it wasn't because of the nurses coming in to check on me or my frequent bathroom visits. Our lack of sleep was mainly due to the incredible, non-stop moaning and yelling of the patient in the room next door. By the sounds of her, you would have thought she was dying, and had she truly been, I would have felt sorry for her but we knew that she was in for a routine "female" procedure and was in no jeopardy of losing her life. As our sleepless hours passed and her hysterics continued, I felt that Bob might indeed sneak into her room and put her out of her imagined misery. Morning arrived and we had barely slept.

Today was Tuesday, September 13th. Bob and I got up feeling as if we had been hit by a Mack truck. Bob because he was dead tired, and me, for the same reason as well as dealing with the effects of my fever. Before Bob left for home, we discussed the fact that I should press either Dr. Wasi or someone of similar ilk, for a timeline for my transplant or at least an alternate plan if Pat was not a match. We had not heard anything from anyone since he had been tested almost eight days ago. In this instance, no news was not good news – it was simply no news and knowing nothing only made our anxiety worse. Every day that went by only inched me closer to the one-month deadline that I had read about in the documentation on aplastic anemia. I knew that as a temporary measure, I could live from one transfusion to the next.

However, I had found out in the past few days that the more transfusions one received, the more antibodies built up in your body and the less receptive you would be to the transplant. In addition, each blood transfusion passed on the donor's iron and this could put you in iron overload! That could also kill you. The only way to get rid of the iron was to do a reverse transfusion and take blood out but, as in my case, if you didn't have that much blood to begin with, then what? I felt that with every method used to prolong my life came an equal or even higher risk of dying.

The same hopeless mood enveloped me as the morning hours passed. Close to noon, my door opened and a young resident whom I had not met before entered and announced that she was here to examine me. Sadly, I cannot remember her name…I'll blame it on the turmoil I was going through. She was a pretty girl, too young looking, I thought, to be a doctor (but then again the older you get the younger those of a lesser age look). She seemed very sensitive and kind and I immediately took a liking to her. She introduced herself and asked me how I was doing. It seemed a humorous question, in a way, considering my condition and prognosis, but I answered her nonetheless and told her I felt like I was stuck to the bed unable to move. I did make her aware that I had noticed a swelling in my genital area that had just started the previous night. It appeared that no part of my body was spared from this disease and its effects. She examined me and decided at this point it was best not to rock the boat and, therefore, would not want to do anything about it for the single reason that she didn't want to "disturb" what was going on and cause an even worse situation. Each diagnosis was about weighing the risks of treatment versus the potential danger of the problem if it was left status quo. The resident continued by asking me the same questions that I had already answered innumerable times. I began to wonder if I even had a chart because no one seemed to be reading it! This feeling of no one knowing me or what was going on suddenly welled up inside me. Why did I have to repeat these same damned things over and over again?

In complete desperation, I looked into her eyes and told her that NO ONE was giving ME any answers and did anyone really know who I was or what I had, because it sure as hell didn't seem like it to me. I was beyond worrying about how I came across and I wanted to be heard! She was taken aback, but I forged on pointing out that I had read that I had four weeks left and the clock was ticking. No one had even bothered to give me an update as to what was going on with Pat's marrow typing! Gasping for breath from the exertion of speaking for so long, I continued by saying that I had the impression that I was a faceless person in an overburdened medical system. I told her my mind was my strength and with no hope, I had nothing.

The young woman looked at me and voiced the phrase that so many of us use without ever really thinking about the meaning of what we are saying: "I know how you feel, Esther." Before she could continue, I looked at her shaking my head and quietly started to cry. I said that NO she did not have any idea how I felt. She was twenty-something and healthy and I was lying in this bed…dying. How could she possibly know how I was feeling? I re-iterated that I had to have something to hang onto in order to want to live. She stopped whatever she was about to say and looked at me earnestly and said, "You are right, I have no idea how you feel, but what I can do is see if I can get some answers to your questions. I promise I will get back to you." I thanked her and said that that was all I wanted.

Alone again in my room, I tried to catch forty winks but with the regular visits from the nurses, that was nearly impossible. Don't get me wrong, I was appreciative that they were taking such good care of me: keeping continuous track of my fever, blood pressure, oxygen, not to mention the morning blood tests as had been done in 3Z. Occasionally, I'd have to make my way to the bathroom which proved fairly difficult, because it entailed taking my pole each time and since it would not fit into that closet-sized room, I'd have to leave it outside. The door had to be kept slightly ajar so that the tubing would not get crushed. Once in the bathroom, I did a balancing act, hovering over the toilet seat in an effort not to make contact with it. I was grateful for the presence of the grab bars next to the toilet because it gave me something to hang onto; otherwise, I would have toppled over because my legs did not have the strength to support me. After each visit, much time was spent washing and rewashing my hands. When lunchtime came, I took my dose of "Swish and Spit," which now had to be taken two or three times during the eating process because my mouth sores were getting worse by the day. Every mouthful of food was a struggle – both mentally and physically – but I tried to eat as much as I could.

Before Bob left in the morning, he arranged for a phone card so that I could use the phone in my room. Even though he had been in touch with my family, I knew my Mom and Pat were eager to hear my voice. In the afternoon, I dialed my Mom's number and she picked up the phone. The voice that said hello sounded like that of a 110-year-old and I had no doubts as to what the cause of her distress was...me. We chatted a bit and I asked her how her visit was going with my Aunt Memke, from Belgium. Mom confirmed what I had thought initially which was that she was grateful to have company during this difficult time otherwise she didn't know what she would have done. Both Pat and Linda worked full time and were unable to be with her during the day so that my aunt's being there was indeed a blessing. After awhile, Mom asked me how I was doing and she knew by my struggling, weak voice that things were not good. I could tell that it was all she could do not to start crying. It was the kind of day where I was baring my soul and Mom was no exception. I told her that at this point I didn't care about my dying but what distressed me the most was what I was putting everyone through. Mom answered that was the last thing I should be worrying about and what I needed to do was focus on having a positive attitude and getting better. I knew she was right and I told her I would give it my best shot. Mom and I had always had this ritual where we could not hang up until we said about 10 goodbyes to each other…I barely managed one, I felt incredibly feeble.

Later in the afternoon, Bob returned. I was always relieved and excited to see him. He was my lifeline and only his strength pulled me out of these recurring feelings of despair. It's not that he didn't feel the same, but he did a good job of appearing strong and confident…most of the time anyway. He told me afterwards, that on many a day he would leave me and cry in the car all the way home knowing that I only had a 30% chance of surviving.

Bob asked me about my day and if I had seen any of the doctors. I told him about my discussion with the resident and he commented that he was very proud of how I had opened up to her about how I felt and what I needed. Now it was time to wait again until the next step. Tomorrow would be eight days since Pat's test and we were all going out of our minds waiting for the results.

That evening, Bob gave me another sponge bath because my room had no shower and I was not allowed to use the common shower area because of my low white cell count, which was just fine with me! Nothing bothered Bob when it came to looking after me: he dealt with my body as if it were his own. Once I was bathed, he found me a fresh hospital gown and clean blanket. In a short period of time, he had learned where all the "good stuff" was in the hospital and had discovered where to find the newer hospital gowns or the heated blankets (if I got especially cold).

I knew, by the way the nurses looked at him, they felt he was a pretty special guy and so did I. Several fellow patients told me later that they knew of couples where the caregiver had flown the coop because they just couldn't deal with the constant stress and pressure. Bob was *not* one of those people…"for better or for worse" was definitely his motto and truthfully, it couldn't get any worse than this…we thought.

To lighten the mood a little, we decided to play a game of Scrabble, which Bob had brought to the hospital. He wheeled my dinner tray close to the bed and placed the wooden tiles on it…the game itself was about 20 years old…practically an antique. The nurses thought that this was particularly sweet given the seriousness of our situation. After we finished our game, Bob set up his cot and we each fell into our beds totally worn out. No sooner had we settled into bed when THE PATIENT in the room next door began wailing and screaming. Most of it had to do with her bedpan and the necessity of either having one brought to her or having it taken away. At one point, I felt that I might be able to muster enough strength to stagger into her room and clonk her over the head with it! Bob and I looked at each other in the semi-darkness and groaned at the prospect of yet another entire night of this. I had not had much hospital experience at this stage of the game, but I knew enough to know that she was making a giant nuisance of herself. Whatever she had wasn't life-threatening but you would have thought that she was dying a painful death. It wasn't often that you saw a nurse lose his or her patience, but this person was getting perilously close to driving them all over the edge. By the time we got up in the morning, she had set a record for being the most obnoxious patient.

Chapter 6

September 14ᵗʰ to September 17ᵗʰ

Instead of leaving, Bob stayed that Wednesday morning in order to accompany me to the Imaging/Diagnostics area, because I had to have some lung X-rays taken to ensure I wasn't developing pneumonia. This was standard operating procedure for people like me whose white cells were virtually non-existent. An orderly was called and once he arrived, he pushed my wheelchair and delivered me to the X-Ray department with Bob following closely behind. I was wrapped in a couple of extra blankets because other than my room, we knew that the rest of the hospital felt like a giant commercial refrigerator most likely on purpose so that only a minimal number of "Super Germs" developed.

When we got to radiology, there were quite a few people waiting, including many young children. One of the hematologists had referred to children as "Snot Pools" and advised that I should avoid them at all costs considering my vulnerability to infections. With this in mind, Bob suggested to the orderly that I be parked well away from the throng and he gladly obliged, asking Bob to contact him once we were finished so that he could deliver me back to my room. It would have been faster and easier for Bob to handle the wheelchair but hospital rules did not allow that. We began to wait and wait and wait. The longer I sat there, the more terrified I became of all the germs around me. With every cough, sneeze and blowing of a nose we heard, Bob and I glanced at each other with fear in our eyes.

Mine were not difficult to read because that was all he could see since I had a mask on. After about 45 minutes, Bob was reaching his boiling point and decided to go to the registration desk and hurry things along. He basically pulled a Shirley MacLaine from the movie *Terms of Endearment* akin to when MacLaine started screaming and yelling at the nurses for more pain killers for her dying daughter. Within five minutes, we were ushered into the X-ray room! A technician placed one of those heavy lead shields on me and my legs nearly buckled at the weight of it. I knew they used these to protect women's ovaries but given my scenario, I thought it somewhat funny at the time. That was the last thing I was worried about! We were done in no time at all and Bob went to the desk to request that the orderly be paged to take us back to the ward. Once again Bob had to get quite vocal because the orderly took forever to arrive. I was relieved to get back to the safety of my room. I continued to empathize more and more with Howard Hughes and his obsession with cleanliness and his own pure environment.

By this time it was almost noon, and as Bob and I were talking, the door suddenly swung wide open and Dr. Wasi and a resident hematologist burst into the room. With a broad smile, Dr. Wasi informed us that my brother Pat was a perfect 6 point match!!!!!!!!!! (I cannot put enough exclamation marks after that one to symbolize how we felt at that moment.) We stared at them…I think my jaw dropped…and I started to cry. These were tears of the purest joy imaginable. Bob was teary-eyed as well and immediately picked up the phone to call Pat and my Mom. Upon hearing the news, Pat began to cry…now he knew he would be able to save my life. My Mom was ecstatic, needless to say. After Bob got off the phone, I looked at the two doctors and still sniffling, said to them that I was indeed the luckiest person on this earth. The resident, who happened to be the one that told Bob I had a 30% chance of surviving a transplant, gave me a strange look knowing what was still ahead. Dr. Wasi on the other hand, showed complete elation because it was not often that she could personally be the bearer of such joyous news. That morning, we did not know or appreciate the rarity that a single sibling could be a match. Apparently, the last time that had happened had been twenty years prior. Later that day we were told that one patient needing a transplant was one of ten brothers and sisters and there was not one match. We felt that we had won the biggest lottery on the planet.

Once we all regained our composure, Dr. Wasi got down to business in terms of what was ahead. Now that we had a match, the transplant was to be scheduled for October 7th which interestingly was two days prior to Thanksgiving Day (in Canada). Dr. Wasi explained several things about the protocol for the transplant. Most importantly, whatever few remaining white cells I had left would have to be completely eradicated so that Pat's bone marrow would be able to engraft without getting into a fight with my immune system; or alternatively, stop my body from rejecting his bone marrow. This would be accomplished by infusing my body with heavy doses of chemotherapy lasting up to 8 hours per day commencing 6 days prior to the transplant and was referred to as the preparative regimen. Transplant day was known as "Day 0" by the medical staff and the days preceding that were numbered "-6, -5, -4," etc. Sort of like a Space Shuttle launch countdown. Similarly, the day after transplant would be called "Day 1" as a benchmark of the waiting period until engraftment took place. Blood work would be done daily each morning while I was receiving the chemotherapy and as soon as my white cell count reached "0," the chemotherapy treatments would be halted after which followed a day of rest and then the transplant itself would be performed. My current white cell count was 0.3 which meant the magic number of "0" was theoretically, not far away.

Because the long doses of chemotherapy posed such a threat to your body, tests had to be performed on various organs prior to the administering of it. These test results would also be used as a baseline for evaluating the function of my organs post-transplant and whether they had been adversely affected by the chemotherapy. Appointments were to be made for me to have chest x-rays, an electrocardiogram, breathing tests and abdominal ultrasounds. Based on the results, the doctors would determine if I was physically strong enough to withstand the strain of the chemo. To quote an information booklet I was given…"The greatest risk of a bone marrow transplant is the procedure." Translation…the cure could kill you!

This was a great deal of information to digest so Dr. Wasi said that her transplant team would see me in the afternoon to give us the rest of the protocol. Now we had a plan and a date…and dare I say it – most importantly…HOPE! Even though the bone marrow transplant was dangerous, it was the only game in town and I was not going down without a fight.

Bob had to leave for home at this point in order to phone and email our friends and tell them the fantastic news. He would return that afternoon and spend the night again. Even listening to the noise from the patient next door wasn't going to quash our good mood.

By mid-afternoon, the transplant team coordinators, Kathy and Tina, came by to give me additional details about the whole transplant procedure. It had been decided that since I was in the hospital anyway, the next two days, Thursday and Friday, would be spent doing the tests I had been told about. Hopefully, provided my fever receded, I would be discharged by Saturday and stay home for fourteen days during which time I would have twice-weekly appointments for transfusions. On September 30th, I would be re-admitted so that the chemotherapy could be administered six days prior to "Day 0," October 7th. They told me that Bob would be able to stay overnight until "Day -1" and then I would be prepared for the bone marrow transplant. Once the transplant was done, I would be in isolation for however long it took for the new bone marrow to engraft. This meant that only the hospital staff and Bob would be able to see me with possibly the odd visitor, providing they were healthy. ALL incoming people had to wear masks. For once, I would not have to worry about wearing one. The room that I would be in for my isolation period contained no shower or bath and thus the only time I would be allowed to leave my room would be to bathe in a segregated shower area across the hall. Great emphasis was put on advising me to wear a mask during this brief exit from my room. Because the shower was used by other people, the cleaning staff disinfected it after each use and once that was done, they placed two large strips of masking tape across the door in the shape of an X and that would be THE SIGN that the room was good to go for the next patient. It reminded me of something out of the Bible.

Having always suffered from claustrophobia, the mere thought of being in one room for as long as a month or maybe more frightened me, but having no alternative I would just have to "suck it up" and deal with it. Now we had discussed a transplant date, the tests beforehand, my admission date and an overview of the isolation period which could last as long as five to six weeks. The length of the isolation depended totally on if and when Pat's marrow would engraft into mine. Because I would be given chemotherapy and countless other fluids and medications simultaneously, a device called a central venous catheter, or Hickman Line would be inserted on admittance day, September 30th. I didn't have a clue what that was, but obviously it was some useful device that had been developed by a person named Hickman. Kathy and Tina explained the catheter to me. It was the "super highway" of catheters as opposed to the two lane country road because it could accommodate numerous drugs going in at once as well as the withdrawal of countless vials of blood for tests…it saved you from becoming a human pincushion during the transplant ordeal. The procedure was to be done under sedation, or general anesthetic, by a radiologist or surgeon. In layman's terms, the catheter would be implanted into a large vein in the chest just above the heart. Two incisions would be made: the first one to accommodate the entry where the catheter would be tunneled into the vein and placed in position; the second incision would be the exit area. The exit incision would be where the lines would come out of my chest and that would be the location from which I would be "fed" all drugs, chemicals, and fluids. Images of an octopus came to mind as I listened. Kathy and Tina further explained that the procedure was not without risk because if the catheter went down the wrong "road," there would be serious or perhaps even fatal complications. The end result was that it was the best venue for receiving the chemo and such and was recommended to all transplant patients. Exceptions were rare. The only choice was whether it was placed in my chest or arm, but the consensus by the team was that the chest location was preferred for me. I had to forget about the danger and just go with it. Determinedly, I signed the release form, handed it to Tina and Kathy and they left.

What a day it had been. My mind was spinning with all the information that had to be absorbed, but the bottom line was I had caught the brass ring today and no one could take that away from me. I was born a Taurus and my inherent determination or stubbornness as some people called it was kicking in…I was going to survive and that was that…provided I could make it to October 7th. That was my biggest fear. I knew I had the resolve to get through the transplant but would some unknown infection kill me before then. I had to hope that modern medicine would keep me alive until "Day 0."

Bob returned later in the afternoon and we were still so euphoric from the day's fantastic news. As he poured himself an extra large plastic cup of chardonnay – after all, he was celebrating! I explained everything that the transplant team had told me during their visit. He was nervous about the Hickman insertion and even though it was dangerous, he knew that it had to be done. He agreed that our biggest forthcoming hurdle would be for me to stay as complication-free as possible until bone marrow transplant day. We hoped that my fever would be gone by Saturday and that I would be discharged to a less germ-riddled environment! A hospital is really the last place you want to be when you are sick. It's not that I was Mrs. Clean at home but these "super bugs" that existed in hospitals were not present in our house, and it would be a safer place to spend the next two weeks. The only bugs we had were real ones like spiders and ants and they were much safer than the invisible ones.

During the evening, Bob phoned my Mom and Pat. Confirming that everyone was of good health, it was decided that Mom, Aunt Memke and Pat would come to visit us in the hospital the following afternoon since we now had something to celebrate. Unfortunately, my sister-in-law Linda could not get away from work since she had just started a new job. I knew her thoughts were with us and that was all that mattered. Bob also had to tell them that there would be no kissing and that they had to wash their hands when they came into the room. I knew they would have all bathed in bleach if it meant seeing me. For a change, I actually looked forward to the next day.

Thursday morning came and Bob packed up his cot once again. I guess the good news about me being sick was that he was becoming very domesticated. While he was finishing tidying up the bedding, my breakfast arrived. Eating meals had not gotten any easier, worse actually because my mouth was now filled with sores and I was so anxiety ridden that I could barely swallow. Regardless of how I felt on both counts, I had my "Swish and Spit" cocktail and ate most of what was on the tray. I was a fairly slim person and could not afford to lose any weight...I had to be fighting fit for what lay ahead.

A couple of hours later, one of my nurses came in and said that I would be heading for a stress test on another floor. I remember thinking that I was living a stress test every second of every day and if I had survived all the strain so far, that had to count for something. One of the stress tests would entail riding a stationary bicycle, which meant I had to change out of my hospital gown and into the clothes that I had worn the day I had been admitted to emergency. Since I did not have running shoes, the nurse said I could wear my slippers. An orderly came by and wheeled me to the elevator and I kept thinking that this was really funny in a sick sort of way. Here I was, heading for a stress test...unable to walk, in a wheelchair wearing sheepskin slippers AND just the act of talking made me breathless. I had to assume that my transplant team knew what they were doing.

When I arrived in the cardiology area, a nurse took over and wheeled me to a secluded hallway where I would be away from the masses. Naturally, I had a mask on, which had become my new best friend. By now I knew that I had to change it every 20 minutes, otherwise there was no point in having it on. After about 10 minutes, another nurse came by and asked me to step on a scale to get my weight and BMI (Body Mass Index), which wasn't much let me tell you. I was so weak that I actually teetered on the scale trying to stay balanced. I could only imagine what a disaster this stress test would be.

As with all the nursing staff, everyone was very considerate and friendly. One of the nurses asked me briefly about my illness and even with her medical background was surprised to hear that I had been stricken with such a rare disease. She knew what I was facing and respected me for the strength that I would need to get through it. Once she had my weight information, she wheeled me into the stress test room and introduced me to another nurse who would be doing the next segment. This included yet another blood sample to give them my hemoglobin count. At first I was pleased that the nurse would get it by using one of those finger lances instead of a needle; however, the lance actually hurt more, but I showed no outward sign of the pain. I was getting used to the discomfort of all of these blood lettings. When she was finished, she tested my blood and informed me that my hemoglobin count was 76 which meant 39 points below the normal low for a woman. I wondered whether perhaps the tests would be cancelled, but orders were orders and there was no veering from this course! Off we headed to the bike where two other nurses took over.

My torso was covered with suction cups attached to electrodes and I was wired to a machine that would monitor my heart and breathing rate while I cycled. I felt a bit like Lee Majors in the "Six Million Dollar Man"…I definitely watched too much TV as a young person! The nurses told me that I would be breathing through a tube inserted in my mouth, and my nostrils would be clamped shut with basically a clothespin so that there would be no cheating by trying to breathe through your nose. LOVELY! The initial phase of my cycling would be set at the easiest resistance. As we worked our way through the test, the nurses would gradually increase the resistance to see how far I could progress. If I made it through a cycle, I would graduate to the next level and so on. During this process, they would watch my vitals and if at any time I began to feel unwell, I would give them the thumbs down sign to stop or thumbs up sign to continue. There was no limit as to the levels to be achieved; it strictly depended on the fortitude of the individual.

While I was being instructed on the procedure of the test, a man had entered the room to also have a stress test done. He was ushered to the nurse who would lance him for a blood sample. As we were focusing on starting my tests, we heard an ear-piercing "YOUCH!" We all looked at each other in that conspiratorial way that only women can, all the while thinking that it was a good thing that men never had to bear children.

Now it was time to start the machine and my test. I was determined to do well in spite of how I felt because I wanted to show my doctors that I was physically able to undergo the transplant. The final outcome was that I made it to level eight which was not too shabby considering I was told that the average person rarely made it to ten. I think the fact that I had always stayed in shape by either exercising or horseback riding was proving to be a benefit. Three years later, I made it to the tenth level.

The next part of the test was to be conducted in an airtight chamber where I would be asked to blow into a machine that would measure my lung strength and capacity. There would be resistance in the tube so that it would be like blowing up a balloon that was trying to blow air back at you. I didn't do as well at that but my score was acceptable considering that just talking was an effort for me. It took about two hours to complete all the tests, after which the nurses wished me good luck and an orderly came to wheel me back to 3Z. I knew I had done quite well with the results of these tests and I hoped that the next set would be as successful.

By the time I got back to my room, I felt as if I had run an Olympic Marathon and was thankful to get into my bed and rest for a while. No sooner had I gotten comfortable than a nurse came in to tell me I was getting a blood transfusion. Obviously, my morning routine blood tests had indicated I was low which I already knew from the lancing in the stress test unit. I was getting used to this whole procedure and the sight of the blood didn't bother me at all any more. Now my thoughts were…"thank goodness someone has donated my blood type and I can live another day!"

In the mid afternoon, Mom, Memke and Pat arrived. It was a poignant moment to see them all and especially Pat because I looked at him in a whole new way. He held my life in his hands. They all wanted to kiss me or at least give me a hug, but that was out of the question because in our minds it was too risky. This was the first time that I had seen my aunt in 12 years and I'm sure that she thought it would be the last. When I glanced at my Mom over the mask, I could see that she was barely able to keep it together but somehow, she managed. I'm sure it was torture for her to not be able to hold me and kiss me; after all that was what mothers did in situations such as these. Pat kept looking at me and his eyes said…."how could this possibly be happening to you?" I must have looked a fright to them lying in bed, hooked up to an IV, and struggling for air each time I spoke. It was admirable that they were able to control their emotions as well as they did; we all knew it would only make matters worse if they didn't. We naturally talked about the miracle of Pat and I matching and we told them about the information we had been given as to the whole transplant process. Bob did most of the talking since I could only speak for short spells at a time. I think they were more overwhelmed than we were. Through our daily exposure to this odd world of blood disorders, we were slowly getting used to its terminologies and protocols.

After an hour and a half or so, they knew I was worn out and they decided to leave. It was a heart wrenching goodbye. Pat and I looked at each other saying nothing. Our new relationship went beyond mere words. My sweet aunt from Belgium said a happy goodbye which belied the look in her eyes. What a shock it must have been to her upon arriving at Mom's to discover that her niece was horribly ill. Memke had always been one of my favorite aunts. I had to give her kudos for being such a trooper. My parents had emigrated from Belgium when Pat (9) and I (7) were kids and we had maintained regular contact with all of our relatives. I had returned to Belgium many times and valued the family ties. Now with the wonders of modern technology and the advent of email and web cams it made that communication all the easier. When it was time for Mom to leave, she could not control herself any longer and she grasped my hand. Somehow, she held back the tears…for a while anyway. As they were leaving, I could see her shoulders heaving up and down and I knew she was already crying and would be doing so most of the way home. As it turned out, the timing of my aunt's visit was a godsend because she provided incredible moral support for Mom during her stay. I felt dreadful for what I was putting them through.

After my family left, I told Bob about my experiences in the cardiology section and the stress tests of the morning. He was not surprised that I had done well and had more or less expected it considering I had always been in good shape prior to my getting sick. That taught me that staying fit was important for many reasons…never would I have imagined that my survival depended on it. Bob was extremely happy and felt it was just one more hurdle out of the way. While Bob ate his pizza and drank his glass of chardonnay, I ate the hospital fare. Unfortunately, the catered vegetarian foods seemed to have disappeared and we were now into more basic choices, none of which were very enticing. At this point, I ate to survive.

The following day, my fever was finally gone and provided my status didn't change, I would be discharged in two days. Bob stayed rather than going home because my next set of tests were in the nuclear medicine section that afternoon. I was to be injected with some kind of nuclear chemical that would show whether everything was working properly in terms of my heart and circulation. There was no point in giving me a transplant if my heart and circulatory system were unable to handle the onslaught of chemo and the other dangerous medications. For a person who had rarely seen a doctor in 48 years, I was making up for lost time and the speed with which this was all happening was overwhelming. Bob walked alongside as I was wheeled to another level of the hospital. The medical personnel in the nuclear section were pleasant and explained what they would be doing. I was to have yet more blood drawn and it would be mixed with some nuclear "stuff" and then I would be reinjected with it. The two doctors would then view a monitor to follow the flow of the nuclear fluid and verify that there were no blockages or potential problems. The entire process took about an hour and at the end of it, I was deemed fit in terms of my circulation and heart. Whether I would glow in the dark as a result remained to be seen. It looked like things were coming together and Bob and I were very happy, or at least, as happy as one could be knowing what still lay ahead. This was a game of inches.

That evening, while we were playing Scrabble, we heard THE PATIENT next door making more than her usual amount of racket. We found out that she was about to be discharged but the person who was supposed to pick her up, had not appeared. There was probably good reason for that! When a nurse came in to check on my vitals, Bob mentioned to her that he would gladly come up with the money for cab fare if it would mean getting rid of her once and for all. The nurse laughed and thought this was quite funny but…Bob was dead serious. We had had it with this woman's crying and complaining and couldn't wait for her to get out of her room and away from us. Finally, about an hour later, someone arrived to get her and a lovely silence descended upon us.

On Saturday morning, September 17th, I was given the go-ahead to return home. Dr. Wasi gave me several prescriptions for medications that would keep my body under control for the next couple of weeks. One of the prescriptions was for a drug called fluconazole. This drug prevented oral and other fungal infections. As I stated before, without a normal immune system your body will begin to develop all sorts of problems, and in my situation such an infection could be fatal.

Driving home was a strange feeling. Each time I left the house, I felt that I would never return and yet, somehow I survived and I would be back home again. It was the non-stop roller coaster ride again. Max, our shepherd, was so delighted at seeing us that he was the proverbial tail wagging the dog. His giant tail was like the propeller on a plane about to take off with his entire body getting into the action. Dudley, on the other hand having a short tail, showed his pleasure by engaging in a canine conversation and yowling as if to say, "Where the heck have you been? I've got so many things to tell you!" Dudley had always held a special place in my heart. I had found him at a breeder's and at the age of 15 weeks had never been chosen because he did not have the attributes of a good hunting dog. His fun-loving personality and sweet face won me over. It warmed my heart to see them. Unfortunately, I couldn't pet them or play with them as I usually did but just having them around me was of great comfort. I thought again how lucky dogs were not to be "smart" enough to know when they were sick or dying. How can I explain what it was like to face death? Countless times I had listened to songs or watched movies about people dealing with a terminal illness and what they would do with whatever time they had left. Invariably, their plans were to travel and do the things they never had the chance to do. Personally, I think that is fairy tale stuff – it's the perspective of a person who has never been in that position. By the time you know you are dying: a) you are probably too sick to go anywhere, and b) you want to be with the ones you love and stay where your soul is comfortable. Perhaps that is just me. What you want to do is live your life *as if you have been diagnosed with a terminal illness*.

Once I was settled in, Bob left to pick up my prescriptions. When he returned home about an hour later, he had an incredulous look on his face. He explained that he had filled the fluconazole prescription and had been told the cost was approximately $80.00. He was a bit shocked at the price considering we had a drug plan and mentioned this to the cashier to which she answered, "Yes sir, we know, otherwise it would be over $800.00." It seemed that these fluconazole pills were the price of gold. I looked at the bottle and I was to take four per day at six-hour intervals. They were small, uncoated pink pills with four sharp edges that stuck very nicely in your throat when you took them. To make matters worse, when they did get stuck, the taste was horrible and, truly, with a name like fluconazole, what else would one expect. I felt many times that the person who designed their shape should have had to take the pills for a day. I had no doubt that the design and taste would have been changed P.D.Q.!

Chapter 7

September 18ᵗʰ to September 26ᵗʰ

Once home, I had a bit more energy now because my fever was under control and the blood transfusions had brought my hemoglobin up to a more normal level. Bob took advantage of my ability to lend a small hand with some minor household chores and he began to mow our acreage and catch up on farm duties. Mike had been helping out with this but with some 13 acres of grass there was still plenty that needed cutting. Bob had always enjoyed looking after our property himself but in this situation, because of his additional house duties, time at the hospital and our business, he had been thankful for Mike's help. Not only was Mike a good friend, but he was also our General Manager in our retail business. Were it not for him and all our wonderful staff who looked after our store during this time, our situation would have been even more difficult to get through. At least we didn't have to worry about our livelihood.

Later that afternoon, Bob prepared my lunch and brought it on a tray to our bedroom. He had done his usual job of making the food visually pleasing and that was always a sweet surprise. Today he had cut a strawberry in the shape of a flower and put it on a small plate. Most people who knew Bob would never have guessed at the tenderness that was hidden beneath that tough exterior. No one could have tried any harder to come up with things that were easy for me to eat as well as being tasty, and considering it all had to be soft and lukewarm, this was not an easy feat. I'm sure he felt as though he were feeding an infant.

The "Swish and Spit" was still a very necessary routine prior to and during eating. For dessert, Bob had decided that a canned product made of Jell-O and fruit was an excellent choice. It would provide some calories and be mushy to eat. Let me tell you this! As a Belgian and the daughter of a chef, canned Jell-O with fruit was not in our repertoire. Growing up, I had always viewed Jell-O as colored blubber but since Bob had personally chosen this I could, and would, turn a blind eye. I imagined it as chocolate mousse!

By Sunday morning, my energy was waning again. Mom had been hoping that she and Memke would be able to visit while I was at home and at the same time, they could offer some domestic help and do the cooking. I had after all, twelve days before I was to be admitted to McMaster again, and once I was in isolation, no one but Bob would be seeing me. This seemed like the perfect time for them to come for a few days as long as they were healthy and Bob arranged to pick them up at a local train station. We hoped no sniffles or sneezes would interfere with their plan to come.

By the time that Mom and Memke arrived, I was virtually bedridden again. I was able to get up for only a few short minutes at a time and then would fall back into bed feeling lifeless. In spite of how I felt, it soothed me to see them and I got a kick out of watching two sisters in their seventies interact. They would chit chat in their native Flemish tongue while cleaning or cooking and act as if they had never been apart. I imagined them as young girls during World War II in Belgium growing up in my grandparents' house where I had been born. What I had initially thought to be terrible timing for Memke's visit now in hindsight couldn't have been better. Bob did have to tell Mom that he planned to continue preparing my meals since he had a better handle on what I could and couldn't eat. As a Belgian mother, this was a difficult thing to understand since the

Belgian culture was all about excellent home cooking, plenty of it and always served scalding hot on a pre-warmed plate. This was the part that Bob was worried about; he knew I could not eat food of that temperature. My Mom took it in stride and said she would prepare some soups for me that would provide nourishment, be easy to eat and Bob could heat it to whatever temperature he saw fit. He knew homemade soups were one of my favorite foods and hoped that would entice me to eat. In the meantime, Bob looked forward to some excellent Belgian cooking. One evening, Bob barbequed hamburgers for himself and the two ladies. My aunt, in all her years, had never eaten a BBQ'd hamburger. She explained that she disliked the taste that charcoal gave to foods. Bob told her that ours was a propane BBQ and no such flavor would be imparted to what he BBQ'd. That night, Memke prepared her burger with every single condiment on the table…it was a tower by the time she finished and she could barely get her mouth open wide enough to take a bite. I took a picture of her eating it and we emailed it to her son in Belgium…he was aghast that his mother had finally eaten a burger after all these years of their trying to persuade her. We had many laughs that night watching her eat. On some evenings, if I had enough energy left at the end of the day, we would all play Rummicub (a sort of card game using plastic tiles instead of cards). It was Memke's favorite game and gave us a chance to share some laughing and teasing in spite of the dark clouds that loomed overhead.

Mom and Memke ended up staying a total of eight days, twice as long as originally intended. It was a trying time for all concerned as each day brought a new and unwelcome health crisis. Of particular discomfort were my hemorrhoids which had gotten so large that each night I had to soak in an Epsom salt solution in a bowl that hooked onto the toilet. For twenty minutes I'd sit on my throne while the warm water mixture worked its magic.

Twice a week, Bob and I would go to the hospital to have my blood work done and depending on the results, I would receive blood and/or platelet transfusions. In addition, the nurses would check my other blood chemistry to make sure that all my organs were doing what they were supposed to be doing. So far, my liver and kidneys were hanging in there but I was consistently plagued by a bladder infection that could barely be kept under control. Dr. Wasi prescribed some super-duper antibiotics that we hoped would get rid of the infection once and for all. I had never realized until this illness how complex a machine the human body was and how many millions of functions it performed daily unbeknownst to me. Somehow I had let my body down and had taken the amazing tasks it did for granted. Now, it was up to my doctors and me to try and keep it going one way or another.

Nightly, Pat and I would talk for an hour or as long as I could last. Linda told me that Pat would pace up and down their hallway or kitchen while we chatted as he tried to work off his tension. We talked mostly about the transplant and how I was feeling. One day we were talking about the excitement of receiving the news that Pat had been a match and we each realized that we had heard "What a Difference a Day Makes" on that very day. There seemed to be something fateful about that song and how it followed me around. Several months later, Pat told me that one night prior to my transplant he had received an alarm call from the retail store where he worked. It was his duty to go to the sight and see why the alarm had gone off. Normally he would have gone but recognizing that if there was a burglary in progress and if he got hurt, it could hamper his ability to be my donor and save my life; therefore he chose not to go. To think how my welfare occupied so many people's minds is still to this day mind-boggling. Pat was upbeat at all times during these conversations and said that his marrow was the "golden juice" and that once I received it, I would be all right. I wished I felt as confident as he did. We knew we didn't have to worry anymore about whether he was a match, but recently I had been given information about something called GVHD and this had me extremely worried. GVHD stands for Graft Versus Host Disease. In short, it means that the incoming bone marrow starts to wage war on any remaining white cells of the recipient. It is in fact an organ rejection because bone marrow is considered an organ. The unusual thing about this type of transplant is that the rejection can show up anywhere and everywhere because the cells that are produced by your marrow "feed" the rest of your organs. Persons receiving a related donor match generally have a lesser chance of getting GVHD, but due to my age and being considered "old" for a transplant, my risk factor was greater than 50% for contracting some form of it. There are two types of GVHD: *Acute* GVHD and *Chronic* GVHD. Acute GVHD – if you were unlucky enough to get it – occurred within the first 90 days following the transplant and was considered very dangerous and perhaps lethal. If you survived the Acute GVHD, you would more than likely acquire Chronic GVHD. Having Chronic GVHD meant you were condemned to a possible lifelong struggle of rejection problems, constantly being managed by some very potent drugs. The prospect of this terrified me but the philosophy in the blood disorder ward was that it was better to live longer with a chronic illness than to die prematurely from no transplant…this was termed the "risk vs. benefit" strategy. We would just have to hope for the best. Pat on the other hand, when I mentioned the GVHD possibility to him would hear none of this negative talk and he just kept saying that all would be well after the transplant and I had nothing to worry about. I always looked forward to our phone calls and through them I felt our bond intensify with each passing day. I should mention that I rarely spoke with Linda, not because she did not want to, but because she wanted me to save what little strength I had so that I would be able to speak with Pat. What she did do was recognize that Bob needed attention too and she made a point of calling him weekly to see how he was doing. Linda is an incredibly selfless, strong person.

When I was feeling somewhat energetic, I would gather paperwork and organize our business bookkeeping so that everything would be looked after during my isolation period and whatever recovery time thereafter. I had notes on my notes and thanks to our efficient office supervisor, Vicki, I felt at least that was something that I would not have to worry about.

In anticipation of my stay in the hospital, Bob had given me a laptop and an iPod. When I wasn't too fatigued, I loaded them with my favorite software, pictures, email addresses and songs. This would be my only connection to the outside world while I was in isolation because we had already decided that we would not allow any visitors, difficult as that might be. One afternoon, while I was updating my laptop, Memke came in and asked me what I was doing. I explained a few things to her but her main focus seemed to be specifically on emailing. Apparently my Mom had been putting the pressure on her so that they could email back and forth once Memke returned home. I think the prospect of being able to communicate with me as well, added some fuel to the fire and upon Memke's arrival in Belgium she asked her son for a computer and learned how to use it. We still email back and forth to this day. She is now 83. So much for the saying that you can't teach an old dog new tricks!

One night, while Mom and Memke were still staying with us, I woke up in the middle of the night with an atrocious taste in my mouth. As I walked to the bathroom to see what was going on, Bob instantly sat up in bed and asked if anything was wrong. His jumping up each time I stepped out of bed had become an ingrained reflex at that point and he still has not broken the habit. I looked in the mirror and I was horrified to see that my gums were bleeding in various locations and what frightened me even more was that I hadn't even been doing anything. Bob immediately phoned 3Z and asked them to page the hematologist on call and since he was not available, we requested a call back. Within a few minutes, the hematologist phoned and Bob worriedly explained what was happening. The doctor asked Bob when our next hospital visit was and coincidentally it was to be that very morning at 10:30 a mere seven hours from then. He told us that more than likely my platelets were extremely low and that was why my gums were bleeding. The gum area was one of the first places to 'let go' when you had no clotting capability. He suggested we stem the flow by packing cotton against any areas that were bleeding and leave that undisturbed for a couple of hours which would hopefully enable some clots to form. He felt that as long as I didn't develop a fever, I would be able to last until my appointment that morning, during which time he was sure they would do a platelet transfusion. It's not that blood was gushing out of my mouth, but the bleeding was steady and slow and since we didn't fully understand the consequences of this, we were both terrified. Now I realize that I would have been fine because my appointment and transfusions were that morning anyway.

Following the doctor's instructions, Bob found some cotton balls and we packed my mouth. It was awful! We tried to go back to sleep but neither of us could. Me, because I had this wet, slimy cotton in my mouth and each time I swallowed I could still taste blood so I knew it had not stopped. Bob, because he was so distraught at yet another crisis that might impede my chances of the transplant going through. The night seemed endless.

At 7:00 a.m., we got up and I couldn't wait to pull out the giant wad of disgusting, blood-soaked cotton. If I didn't get rid of it soon, I surely felt that I would throw up or even worse choke on it. As we pulled the cotton out we saw some clots had adhered to it but with the dislodging of the clots, the bleeding began again. Too late we realized we should have left the packing undisturbed….lesson learned. In a panic, we re-packed my mouth and hurriedly prepared to go to the hospital. Mom and Memke looked somewhat dazed and confused as Bob tried to explain what that day's emergency was and I'm sure they longed to be in a less stressful environment…me, too. I wanted to run away from myself.

When we got to the hospital, on went the mask and Bob got me a wheelchair and we headed directly to the 3Z Outpatient Day Care Room. Once you were in my condition and had an upcoming transplant, you no longer had to go to the public laboratory to have your blood drawn. I guess we had graduated to the "in crowd" and what I would have given to be on the "outs." As we made our way to 3Z, I made a mental note of people's reactions upon seeing someone in a wheelchair. You become invisible. Most people don't want to look at you or, worse yet, be put in a position where they actually have to speak to you. You might as well have the plague. I think that everyone, once in their lifetime, should spend a day in a wheelchair to get an idea of what it is like. For starters, perfectly healthy people wouldn't be taking up handicapped parking spots and people in general would be more helpful and friendly. Case in point…not too long ago I went grocery shopping. This grocery store is built in a bit of a wind tunnel area and typically, my groceries go flying out of the cart once I get outside the door. On this particular day, the winds were extremely high and on my way in, I noticed a man in a wheelchair coming out. There were people scurrying past him in either direction and when I looked at him, I noticed that his Tilley hat had blown off his head and he was trying to grab it which was a problem since the man had no fingers. Without success he was attempting to grasp his hat string between his chin and neck before the hat blew away. I stepped in front of him and asked whether he needed any help and he gratefully nodded. I took his hat, put it back on his head and tightened the string under his chin all the while chatting about what an awfully windy day it was. At this point, albeit too late, several people noticed this man's predicament and saw that I was helping. I felt gratified that I had been able to lend a hand and wondered why people were so busy with their own lives that they could not or would not open their eyes to what was going on around them.

When we arrived in the Day Care room, the nurses drew my blood, took my vitals and asked me how I was doing. Because I had a mask on, they hadn't realized that my mouth was stuffed with cotton and I was unable to speak. Bob told them that my gums had been bleeding most of the night and obeying the hematologist's instructions, we had packed my mouth. He asked if we could take out the cotton and you could imagine my dismay at being told that it would have to stay in until I finished receiving a platelet transfusion. To make matters worse, the results weren't even in yet and the transfusion couldn't start until then. I sat there with a mouthful of swollen, slimy, bloody (literally and figuratively) cotton in my mouth from 7:00 o'clock in the morning until about 1:00 p.m. unable to speak, drink or eat. Oh yes, I could swallow but trust me, THAT was not pleasant. Repeatedly, the phrase "ignorance is bliss" comes to mind. This was one of many occasions during my whole transplant experience when I was thankful that I did not know what each day would bring. Once my second unit of platelets had been transfused, the nurses told me I could take the cotton out which took me all of one second to do. I felt as if I had been liberated from hell and couldn't wait to get the repulsive taste out of my mouth. The good news was that the bleeding had stopped, for now anyway, and we could go home with another disaster under control.

Over the next few days, Mom and Memke stayed busy with cooking and housekeeping. Mom prepared a variety of gourmet, freezer meals intended to keep Bob going while I was in isolation. She made a Belgian sort of Beef Bourguignon which was one of Bob's favorites as well as chili and the like, all in one-portion sizes. At least there would be some quick, delicious meals in the house for him and I hoped that he would take the time to eat them. Having Mom and Memke breathed some life into our home which Bob appreciated because it sure as heck wasn't coming from me. How I wished that their visit could have been under different circumstances, but that was not reality – and this was.

With each passing day and each new complication it became increasingly difficult to remain optimistic that I would stay strong enough to undergo my transplant on October 7th. All I wanted was to make it to THE DAY; once there, I knew I had a fighting chance. Daily, I continued to stare at the photo of Pat and me that was taped to my mirror; only now, instead of wishing him to be a match, I was willing his bone marrow to engraft into my body once transplanted. It was not a given that that would happen just because he was an excellent match: numerous obstacles and curve balls could still come our way. Several evenings during this time, Bob would get very emotional and on occasion he would take me in his arms and start crying. Even though he knew that Pat was a match, he remembered what the resident had told him and knew that my chances of surviving the transplant were only 30%. Because I didn't know this at that time, I felt he was giving up on me and I'd think to myself, "Hey, I'm not dead yet…let me prove how tough I can be." Frankly, it would be a miracle if I survived what was still to come.

Chapter 8
September 27ᵗʰ to September 28ᵗʰ

Mom and Memke left on Tuesday, September 27ᵗʰ. We said a teary goodbye at the local commuter train station and my heart ached as we left and I watched their solitary figures standing on the platform. Once underway, we drove to a scheduled appointment with an OB/GYN that Dr. Wasi's team had made for me. This was standard operating procedure for any woman about to undergo a bone marrow transplant and the specialist's role was to explain the dangers of the chemotherapy on my female anatomy. Somehow I already knew that the bottom line of the whole scenario would be that chemo was not a good thing for your organs…gee, what a surprise!

When we arrived in the parking lot, I waited in the car while Bob went into the building to advise the doctor's office that I was outside and would stay there until my appointment time. We felt it best for me to remain isolated because we knew the waiting room would be filled with women and children as is typical of such a practice. At precisely noon, we entered the waiting room, me with my mask on, of course. Everyone in the room turned to look at us while we stood and waited in the hallway in order to keep a safe distance from them all. I always had the impression that people thought that because I had the mask on that I was the one that had some highly contagious disease as opposed to the other way around. Mostly, I felt like a leper in these situations. Soon the room regained its dynamics with children playing and mothers noisily sharing stories of how

Sarah or Jimmy excelled in their grades. Sometimes I was envious of people whose lives held no complications…dare I say, even jealous.

Within a couple of minutes, a nurse ushered us into one of the many examination rooms and the doctor entered shutting the door behind her. She was a pleasant enough woman but as with so many in her field of OB/GYN, she had a long list of patients and I felt a bit of a number. More than likely, I could attribute that feeling to my state of mind at the time…hard to say. My chart had been sent over from the hospital and as Dr. OB/GYN reviewed it, she commented that it was not often she saw a patient with aplastic anemia. We all concurred that it was definitely not a run-of-the-mill disease.

The pleasantries were kept to a minimum for all our sakes and she immediately got down to the meat and potatoes of the matter by telling me that the chemotherapy would render me sterile and bring on menopause. I told her that neither of these things would cause me any psychological trauma because my tubes had been tied 15 years previous and I had already been in perimenopause for four months now. She nodded in answer and went on to say that once I had the transplant, I would come back to her for a check up after 90 days to see whether I was developing GVHD in my vaginal area. This revelation took me a bit by surprise but I guess it shouldn't have because GVHD could show up anywhere – so why not there? When we said goodbye, she wished me luck and that she would see me in three months but I had the distinct impression that it was only verbiage and she wasn't really expecting to lay eyes on me again. One can only imagine how many bone marrow transplant patients she had seen and what percentage of them had actually survived in order to make a follow-up appointment.

The following day, September 28th, our transplant coordinators had set up a family meeting to be held in a conference room in

3Z. Its purpose was to talk to the involved family members and explain the risks of what I would be facing and give a timeline as to the protocol and recovery. We had decided that the meeting would be too much for my mother to bear and that only Bob and I, and Pat and Linda should attend. The less Mom knew of the perils I would be faced with, the better. Taking time off from work, Pat and Linda met us at the hospital and we were settled into the meeting room for a 1:00 p.m. start along with several people which only reconfirmed the organization and skill that it took to put something like this together. In attendance from the hospital were: Dr. Wasi, Kathy and Tina (the transplant coordinators) and Maggie (the social worker). There was a slide projector and screen set up and something told me it was not to see family vacation photos.

The meeting started with Dr. Wasi welcoming us all. She told us that we would be seeing a slide show that would explain the transplant protocol from start to finish and she encouraged us to ask questions or voice any concerns during the presentation. The show lasted about 40 minutes and didn't leave much to the imagination. To quote my email at that time to our friends describing the meeting…"Basically, it was a slide show of yet again all the wonderful things that will probably, likely, definitely, or maybe happen to me." It included mention of possibly needing a feeding tube depending on how much damage the chemotherapy would do to my throat and mouth tissue. If my urinary tract was affected and I was unable to urinate, a catheter would have to be inserted. Lack of activity during isolation could bring on pneumonia and I could end up in ICU…the possibilities were endless and I kept thinking…"and why again am I doing this?"…"oh yes, there is no choice." We were given a timetable that detailed week by week, what would be happening both from a physiological and psychological standpoint based on 25 years' worth of transplant data. It showed which weeks were expected to be the worst, or the nadir, and gave an idea of when the recovery phase might begin. Dr. Wasi also gave a rudimentary explanation of GVHD and its likelihood post transplant given my age and match. At last, all topics had been covered and looking around the table, she asked if anyone had any questions. Bob asked for more detail on the GVHD issue. This was what I was most afraid of, besides bleeding to death, and I imagined pressing my fingers to my ears saying La La La La La in an effort not to hear. Once that was addressed, there was dead silence in the room with not a movement made by anyone. I turned to Dr. Wasi and said, "OK so much for the good news, what's the bad news?" I gathered that in these situations not many people cracked a joke because everyone just sat there until I said "I was just kidding" and then even only a bit of controlled laughter surfaced. Having lightened the mood slightly I got back to business and while I looked at all the faces, but primarily Dr. Wasi's, I said, "I know that because of my age I am considered not to have much of a chance to survive this. However, let me tell you that even though my birth certificate states that I am 48 years old, my mind and body say I am 38 and that puts me into a different category with less risk of dying and that is how I am looking at what is ahead. I have always been healthy, eaten well and exercised and that has to count for something." The medical team said nothing in response…they dealt with facts which didn't necessarily substantiate what I had just said but I knew that they silently hoped I was right. Many times after my transplant, Dr. Wasi confirmed that being healthy and fit prior to my transplant played a major part in my success afterwards. My biggest council to people is…stay fit because some day you may need your body and if you haven't looked after it, it won't be there for you.

After the meeting, Bob, Pat, Linda and I took a few minutes to have a coffee on the main floor where we discussed how we felt about everything that had been said. We all agreed that it had been the right decision not to include Mom in the proceedings and felt that she would fare better knowing only the barest of details. Pat mentioned that as part of the routine preparation for the transplant, and as a final safeguard, he was to be examined in the next couple of days by one of the hematologists in order to confirm that he was healthy and had no viruses or illnesses that could be passed on. I'm not sure what we would have done if there had been anything and I thanked my lucky stars when Pat called to let me know he had passed with flying colors. When we said goodbye, I hugged Pat with all the strength I could muster wanting him to know how much I appreciated what he was doing for me...I could think of no words to fully express how I felt. The next time I would see him would be on "Day 0."

Thursday was spent sending my last few emails from home and putting the finishing touches on my laptop and iPod. The day had a dreamlike quality to it... we were terribly afraid of the future but yet, we knew it had to happen in order for me to have a chance at life. Strangely enough, I was feeling as healthy as could be expected and for the moment, I had no infections or problems which considering the circumstance was as much as one could hope for. I packed a duffle bag with some toiletries and make-up and whatever other items I thought would be useful. Bob had asked Vicki to shop for some pajamas and she had outdone herself by finding three sets in various colors that mixed and matched with tops and bottoms. I had never had such nice sleepwear in my life because I had always used old T-shirts. That evening, I talked to Mom, Pat and Linda since it would probably be a while before I would be able to speak with them again anticipating that I would be incommunicado during my week of chemotherapy. Pat was his usual positive self and in contrast, Mom sounded frightfully frail...I knew she was barely hanging on emotionally.

Bob and I spent the evening quietly enjoying our home, our dogs but most of all, one another's company. We didn't discuss the "what ifs," there was no point in dwelling on that now, we knew there were difficult times ahead and we would deal with them as they surfaced. Bedtime came with some trepidation knowing that morning would soon follow bringing with it whatever lay in store for us.

Chapter 9

September 29th to October 6th

Dawn arrived and I woke up in that blissful state between semi-consciousness and consciousness where for a few fleeting seconds, my brain had yet to realize that I was terminally ill and about to face a bone marrow transplant. As reality set in, my stomach instantly felt as if I had swallowed a lead balloon and I could feel my abdominal muscles constricting. This had become my usual feeling upon waking up since my diagnosis and once that sensation arrived there was no getting rid of it other than falling into a sleepy oblivion. I wondered if the lead balloon would ever disappear…it still surfaces on occasion when I have any kind of a health challenge.

Bob and I drove to McMaster so that I could be admitted at 9:00 a.m. as per their instructions. Everyone in 3Z commented on how well I looked and I figured it had to be the make-up, nonetheless, I took the compliment as a positive sign that perhaps things would be all right after all. I met one of the many day nurses who would be looking after me over the next few weeks and she showed me to my room where a student nurse was instructed to help me fill out the admittance forms. I had forgotten that this was a teaching hospital and now that fall was here and a new semester had begun, there were a few newbies present under the tutelage of several senior nurses. I wondered if they knew what they were getting themselves into! We once again filled out forms for the hospital kitchen so that hopefully my meals would be vegetarian…I wasn't holding my breath remembering the last time I had been in and the inconsistencies of what I had been served. When the rest of the forms were completed, I changed out of my street clothes, hung them in the small closet and put on a hospital gown wondering when the next time would be that I would be wearing those same clothes. (I didn't want to think about the "if".) I placed my new pajamas in my nightstand drawer having decided not to wear them until after the Hickman was in place. Once Bob knew I was settled in, he left for home and would return at 4:00 p.m. There was no point in him staying for the Hickman procedure since he was not allowed to be present anyway.

At about 11:30 a.m., my nurse brought in a small bag of Benadryl (to avoid any allergic reactions) and two units of platelets to be transfused prior to heading to radiology for the insertion of the Hickman. Apparently, the surgeons in radiology did not want to do surgery on any patient such as myself that had a less than 100,000 platelet count and I knew that mine was well below that. The normal platelet count for a woman is between 150,000 and 400,000. The additional units of platelets would minimize the risk of bleeding since three incisions did have to be made. Unfortunately, there was nothing that could be done to reduce the chances of an infection from the surgery itself...we would keep our fingers and toes crossed. I hoped that everyone scrubbed their hands until there was no skin left! The only sedation I would have was the effects of the Benadryl which made me feel like I'd had two martinis and I didn't even drink martinis. It was not a pleasant sensation and I could barely talk or think after I received it. While I was receiving the Benadryl and then the platelets, I thought about what Janet and I had discussed regarding meditation techniques and I knew that I would need to use them during the Hickman operation and any other challenging times ahead. Being a bookkeeper, I devised my own system using numbers, whereby I would start doing simple calculations. For example, $100 - 8 = 92 + 5 = 97$, and so on. This would, with any luck, keep my brain occupied enough to squelch any thoughts of pain, nausea, or whatever. So far, I had not needed this technique, but I knew that the upcoming procedure and the forthcoming week would probably require it. I had no idea what to expect in terms of the Hickman other than I knew it was dangerous. Ignorance is bliss once again.

After my transfusions, an orderly was called and remaining in my bed, I was rolled down to radiology which was, of course, in the basement. Was there anything not in the basement in this hospital???? When we reached radiology, I was put in a small cubicle surrounded by curtains and a male nurse came in to let me know that they would be ready for me shortly. I noticed he was wearing the identical iPod to the one that Bob had just given me and we talked for awhile about the features that he liked or didn't like. It was pleasant to have a conversation with someone about something other than my illness and predicament. Within a few minutes, another nurse joined us to announce that the surgeon was ready and I could be brought in now.

I was taken into the operating room where there was a surgical team dressed in scrubs awaiting my arrival. The sight of the room and the team frightened me because somehow I had not thought of this as a "real" operation and now what was facing me suddenly hit home. They carefully lifted me onto the operating table. Suspended from the ceiling was a large, spherical, metal object reminding me somewhat of the U.S.S. *Enterprise* from "Star Trek." The side that looked down on me was flat. Once I was organized on the operating table, the surgeon informed me that I would be lying on my back with my face turned sharply to the left away from the area where the incisions would be made and then the cylindrical object would be lowered onto the right side of my face so that I would be unable to move. Basically, my head would be in a vice. Being satisfied that I could not move, oxygen tubes would be placed in my nostrils and then a sheet put over my head so that not even a stray hair could contaminate the surgical site. I would be in this position for approximately 45 minutes and I willed away feelings of overpowering claustrophobia.

Prior to starting, the surgeon began to explain that he would be freezing the skin above and below my right breast where he would be making the entry and exit incisions. He warned me that once he began to "worm" the catheter into the major vein, I would feel the movement because that area would not be frozen. This seemed as good a time as any to start counting; otherwise, I planned to jump off the bed and run away...except of course, I couldn't. With the vice in place, the tubes up my nostrils and a sheet over my head, the surgeon inserted the needle (100-12=88) and began the freezing. (195-11=184) I then felt the sensation of being cut without the pain (77+3=81...no 80). He commented that he would start pushing in the tubing and I was not to move under any circumstances or else things could become really ugly. (80-15=what the hell!) All of a sudden, there was a rather slow mouse working its way through my chest and I thought that this put a whole new meaning to roto-rootering. It is not that it was painful, but the strangeness of the feelings and the knowledge that it was happening so close to my heart was enough to make me want to hightail it out of there. Now I knew the main function of the vice...prevention of my escape. As I kept trying to count and recount, my concentration waned and my total focus was on the weird sensation of the catheter working its way across my chest and the discomfort of the vice pressing my head onto the operating table. My nostrils were so dry from the oxygen I could barely breathe from the pain and it was all I could do not to scream and ask to be released. At long last, the 45 minutes was over – it may as well have been 45 hours for that is what it seemed like – and I heard the surgeon say that they were about to pull out the catheter through the exit incision and then they would suture me up. Looking back, it was perhaps one of the worst experiences of my life...maybe because I hadn't known what to expect and what it would feel like. I have discussed the Hickman with other patients and some said they had no problems with having it put in, but it was worse for them when it came out. The Hickman was to stay in for 100 days or for as long as you had to have multiple medications administered. I already wasn't looking forward to its removal.

After the operation, the oxygen tubing was pulled out and the vice lifted from my head and the relief was incredible. My neck was so sore from having been immobilized for that period of time that I didn't think I would ever be able to move my head in the opposite direction again. I noted that I had no pain, no doubt due to the local freezing where the incisions had been made. An orderly was called to return me to 3Z and I could hardly wait to get back to my room and see radiology in the "rear view" mirror. As I was being rolled along the hallways and into the elevator, I thought that perhaps I should work on honing my concentration techniques...so much for that first effort. No sooner was I in my room than one of the nurses came in to take my vitals and I was amazed that my blood pressure wasn't through the roof. After the nurse left, I was content to rest for a while and looked forward to seeing Bob. Wait until I told him what a horrific experience that had been!

After about an hour of solitude and much needed sleep, my nurse returned as I was waking up and I commented that my chest felt wet. The look on her face was one of shock and following her eyes I looked down at the front of my hospital gown only to gasp at the sight of my chest. I was covered in blood. It looked as if I had been in the final shootout with Bonnie and Clyde. She said that one of the incisions must have started bleeding and she hurriedly left the room to confer with someone. I sat there completely and utterly terrified thinking that indeed I was going to bleed to death after all and I wouldn't even make it to the transplant. My nurse returned shortly and it was decided that a weight, namely a bag filled with water, would be applied to the incision area with the purpose of stopping the bleeding. While all of this chaos was going on, my dinner arrived which was a fairly tasty looking East Indian lentil dish that under normal circumstances I would have been pleased to be served; however, there was no way I could eat anything considering how upset I was over being drenched in blood! Despite how I felt, the nurse insisted I eat because I had to keep my strength up and obediently I complied even though it seemed that I would choke on each and every forkful.

This was the scene that awaited Bob as he walked through my door. "What the hell is going on here?" he cried in disbelief. When he had left me in the morning all had been well and now here I sat covered in blood with a bag of water lying on my chest. I told him that obviously I must not have received enough platelets before my surgery and now one of my incisions had started to seep and wouldn't stop. Hopefully, the weight of the bag would produce a clot and the bleeding would cease. To say we were terrified would be the understatement of the century. Perhaps if I had been able to change into a clean gown, I would have felt better but until the bleeding stopped, nothing could be disturbed for fear of dislodging a clot that might be forming. Every time I looked down at myself, I was petrified. All Bob and I could think of was that I was going to bleed to death. My dream seemed to be coming to fruition.

After about an hour, with the bleeding still going strong, I began to feel nauseated and I told Bob I was about to throw up. No sooner had he scrambled for a bowl, that my lentils came back. Lentils going in are not pretty and let me tell you, coming out they are worse. All I could think of was that I knew I shouldn't have eaten and I should have stood up for myself with the nurse. Lesson learned once again. Bob was so upset…there I was with blood all over me and now …lentils. He cleaned me up as best he could but could do nothing about my blood soaked gown. When the nurse returned, she admitted that the weight was not stopping the bleeding and suggested another plan of attack which was for Bob to apply pressure on the wound and hopefully, that would "stem the tide." In the meantime, Bob had demanded that a surgeon be called from radiology because he felt that I needed another suture to help stop the bleeding that had now been going on for two hours with no lessening in sight. Out of the blue, my body was consumed with severe chills and when the nurse took my temperature, she informed us that I had developed a fever guessing that it was no doubt due to some secondary infection. Things were getting worse by the minute, if that were even possible! I was covered with five heated blankets and my body was still reacting as if it were naked in a -50°F wind chill in Alaska. Soon I began to convulse every few seconds with extreme jabbing pains in my abdomen that with each spasm left me feeling as if I had been punched in the stomach. During all of this, Bob was continuing the pressure on the wound. When the nurse took my temperature again it had taken another hike and was above 103°F and she said that if we did not get it down somehow, I would end up in ICU! Once in ICU, given my state, my chances were not good. It was decided that Bob would be my nurse for whatever time necessary and the nurses would come in for regular checks. For the next four hours, Bob sponged me down with ice-cold water using his left hand and with his right hand pressed on the area that was bleeding. While all of this was going on, the surgeon that Bob had requested, finally came to see me. He said that the appropriate number of sutures had been used and that it was because of my low platelets that the bleeding was seeping through. Bob asked why he could not put in another stitch and he answered that he was afraid to because that could introduce more bacteria and cause an even larger infection than what was already going on. He said for Bob to continue applying the pressure and if, in another two hours the bleeding was still not stopped he would add a suture as a last resort. After the surgeon left, Bob continued to apply pressure and sponge me off. His sponging hand was totally shriveled from the water as well as blue from the cold. Each time he put the cold water on me it would bring on more convulsions and between that and the bleeding I was convinced I was going to die that night. At about 11:00 p.m., the bleeding slowed down and the area began to form a clot. I still had the fever, but it, too, was beginning to drop off with the help of regular doses of Tylenol. It seemed I had dodged a bullet and I would not be heading to ICU after all. Bob was at this stage beyond exhaustion both from stress and physical exertion. Knowing that I was out of the woods he said that if he did not go to bed, he would pass out where he stood. The nurse placed the basin with cold water and several face cloths next to my bed where I could reach it and continue applying cold compresses to my forehead since my head still felt like it was burning off. At least the excruciatingly, painful convulsions had ebbed.

You may be wondering as you read this, why did Bob look after me and not one of the nurses? Well, sadly, there are only two nurses on night shift looking after as many as 12-15 chronic patients. There is no time for one nurse to sit with one patient for five hours. If Bob had not been there, I know I would have ended up in ICU and what would have happened from there, no one will ever know. I have since said that Pat saved my life with his marrow, but Bob saved my life by making it possible for me to make it to the day of the bone marrow transplant.

By Saturday morning, the fever had gone and the bleeding had stopped. It was the calm after the storm and we looked and felt as if we had been put through the proverbial wringer. Bob helped me get out of that bloody gown and washed me down. I never thought I would appreciate putting on hospital garb and even a Versace gown couldn't have felt more luxurious! While I was changing, I couldn't figure out why my stomach muscles hurt so badly and then I realized that it was from all of the convulsions the previous night...I could think of better ways to get a "6-Pack!" After I was cleaned up and had a bite of breakfast, Bob left for home and would return later in the afternoon. While he was gone, the results came in from that morning's blood drawing, indicating that I was in desperate need of a blood transfusion, which didn't surprise me in the least considering how much blood had flowed out of me the previous night. I had hoped that I would not need another transfusion this soon since I did not want to build up any more antibodies that might inhibit engraftment, but there was no choice. I was also told that the timeline for the beginning of the chemotherapy treatments had been moved up and it would commence that afternoon. I sat there in a daze, reeling from the events of the past 12 hours.

I was awaiting my first treatment of chemotherapy as Bob walked into my room in the afternoon. When the nurse came in with the glass bottle, I was taken aback to see that she was wearing a protective gown over her uniform along with goggles and long rubber gauntlets. I recall thinking: You look like you are about to walk into a biological warfare zone and I'm sitting here with a mere hospital gown on about to have THAT injected into me! What is wrong with this picture? As she hooked the chemo up to one of my tentacles, neither Bob nor I looked at each other, acting nonchalant as if this had been done a million times before. RIGHT! We had to be one another's strength.

When she started the flow of the chemo, I tried to concentrate on the fact that in the long run, this would help me survive and pushed aside the fear of the havoc it could wreak on my body. Strangely and ironically certain people who have received chemotherapy as a treatment for various forms of cancer can, over the long term, develop aplastic anemia which is the reason they were using it in this case: *to kill any remaining bone marrow.* One of the first questions I had been asked by Dr. Wasi's team upon being admitted initially to the hospital was whether I had ever received chemotherapy and they were extremely surprised when I had answered that I had not. At least that would have given them a possible reason as to why I developed aplastic anemia.

As I sat there watching the chemo drip into me, I thought about a paragraph that a dear friend of mine had composed and emailed to me. She felt that the imagery of it would help how I viewed the infusion of the chemotherapy and the transplant thereafter. The following is quoted directly from her email.

"Now I'll leave you with my imagery for you …a raging forest fire is about to overtake your immune system. It will appear to lay waste to all life within. But then a deluge of life-sustaining rain will come. Very shortly you will see first one green shoot poke forth, then a sapling will grow, and in time, the whole forest will grow dense and lush, filled with healthy trees that are stronger than ever. The creatures will return, the birds will sing, and life will be beautiful again."

Certainly, the chemo was the raging fire and barring anymore unforeseen catastrophes, I would survive long enough to receive the life-sustaining rain. I printed that paragraph and took it with me to the hospital and read it countless times while I was waiting for Pat's marrow to engraft.

Now that my first infusion was underway, I thought about the upcoming week and the dangers it held for me. The chemotherapy was to be administered for five consecutive days lasting 8 hours per day to be followed immediately by another drug called Atgam for an additional 6 hours therefore, my system would be bombarded for a total of 14 hours per day. The purpose of the Atgam was to suppress my immune system to make sure that no lingering white cells were generated prior to transplant. During the family meeting, I had been told that there was a choice of Atgam which was derived from horse serum, or Thymoglobuline, which came from rabbit serum. When asked whether I had a preference between the two, it seemed only fitting given our lifelong passion with horses, that I choose the Atgam since it came from an equine friend. Maybe it would bring me good luck.

After a short period of time, my lead nurse, (so named because each nurse was assigned one bone marrow transplant patient and they would be solely responsible for the chemo and the eventual bone marrow transfusion) being satisfied that I was under no physical duress, said she would return regularly to check on me. I fully understood that I was not the only patient in that ward that needed attending to. I looked at the pole next to my bed where the bottle of chemo hung and counted the bags on the "tree" as the medicine pole was lovingly referred to. There was a bag of saline which ensured that the chemo was speedily flushed through your system since the doctors wanted it to do as little damage as possible to your kidneys and liver. Next to that hung a bag with antibiotics which would keep any infections at bay. Another bag contained something that prevented blood clots from forming. In addition, there was an odoriferous drug called Cyclosporin which also suppressed the immune system and when you smelled it you would swear there was a skunk in the room. My tree was a veritable smorgasbord of fluids and I found it truly mind-boggling that all of these things were meant to keep me alive, not to mention that they were all attached to my chest via the central catheter. I think that the Hickman could accommodate as many as six tubes at once and in some instances, certain drugs were channeled through the same line because they were compatible and could be administered together. Others, like the chemotherapy or Atgam or Cyclosporin, had to have their own dedicated line. At one point during the ensuing days, an additional IV had to be inserted in my hand because there were not enough tubes to supply what the medical team needed to administer. I kept thinking what an amazing procedure this was and how many transplants had to have been performed to get the protocol to this level. Sadly, I also thought of all of the people who hadn't made it and whose transplant experience contributed to the evolution of a bone marrow transplant. Would I be one of the lucky ones?

That night, Bob stayed again and would be allowed to for the next four nights until the day before my transplant. By day three of the chemo treatments, I was constantly vomiting and when Bob was there, he would spend his time running for a plastic bowl which sometimes arrived in time and sometimes not. These plastic receptacles were a shade of blue that Martha Stewart would have abhorred and they were referred to as "Blue Ware." At one point, there was so little left to throw up I thought surely my toes would come out of my mouth!

When Bob wasn't doing that, he was helping me to the bathroom because I had to urinate constantly due to the large quantity of saline fluid they were pumping through me. Strangely enough, we had to keep track of the amount of urine so that the "out" could be balanced with what I was getting "in" whether it was orally or via IV. They had a gizmo which resembled a measuring cup that fit onto the toilet seat and I would pee into that. Once the measurement had been taken, it would be logged on a sheet of paper and tallied to make sure that everything was moving through properly. After it had been logged, Bob would empty and rinse the container for the next visit and I often wondered how many husbands would be doing that?? During one of Dr. Wasi's afternoon rounds she stopped by to tell me that I was doing a perfect job of my "ins and outs." Upon seeing my quizzical look she explained that what I was urinating equaled exactly what I was taking in and THAT made everyone very happy!

In spite of the well-balanced ins and outs, my body did swell up so much so that my pajama bottoms barely fit and I could hardly believe that this was me when I looked in the mirror. I didn't dwell on it because at that point I was nauseated twenty-four hours per day and how I looked was the last thing I worried about. All I wanted was not to be nauseated. Whatever efforts I had previously made to eat were now completely gone and this brought on great worry for Bob, the nurses and the doctors. My nausea became so all encompassing that even the sight of the menu when left on my bed tray, brought on gagging. Concerned that I did not have much to lose in the way of extra body fat, the nurses enlisted the help of the hospital nutritionist to talk with me about food choices and what would entice me to eat. The worried dietician tried to suggest a variety of things, such as the canned liquid supplement "Ensure" and other high calorie drinks of that sort. My problem was that my sense of smell had become so acute (typical of chemo patients) that I could smell absolutely everything – even the metal cans that the "Ensure" came in. Especially nauseating were warm foods that emitted an aroma (or stench as I thought of it then) which included Bob's coffee or nightly pizza and he had to cease eating anything hot in my room. At least his chardonnay didn't produce an odor and he could consume that with me present. One of the recommendations that the dietician made which did appeal to me somewhat was that she could special order a cold salad for me consisting of crunchy, raw vegetables such as broccoli, cauliflower and cherry tomatoes with crackers and cheese on the side. Agreeing to that, she notified the hospital kitchen of the menu change and arrangements were made that I would be served this for both lunch and dinner. It was as good as it was going to get considering I didn't want to eat anything.

During these few days prior to my transplant, I had no interest – let alone ability – in communicating with anyone. I did make one exception on my second day of chemotherapy, October 2nd because it was Pat's 50th birthday and I phoned to congratulate him on his significant day. I couldn't bring myself to utter the words "happy birthday" because seriously, how happy could it possibly be? I also knew that a party had been planned for him, but when my illness had been diagnosed and the prognosis spelled out, all celebrations had been cancelled. I had quite a bit of guilt over ruining his birthday but I knew that I was the only one fretting over *that* detail. Everyone's focus was on the transplant and my survival.

The following days of chemo took their toll on me and it was all I could do to get out of bed and go to the bathroom, especially with my tree in tow and the weight of the countless bags of medication suspended from it. At one point, one of the hematologists had come in and said that I won the award for most bags...12 bags to be precise. Somehow I didn't feel that holding the hospital record for that was something to be proud of.

What Bob and I would have killed for, was a full night's sleep and I wondered if I had ever slept longer than 60 minutes at a time? That was a distant memory. If I wasn't throwing up or going to the bathroom or being visited by my nurse every two hours, the sensors that kept track of the flow of drugs would start screeching to let the nurses know that they needed attending to. Numerous times they would just go off because an air bubble had developed in the line which blocked the flow of whatever fluid it was monitoring. Not surprisingly, Bob quickly learned how to "flick" the tubing to get the bubble out so that the sensor would stop screaming. We both began to hate these machines even though we knew they were a necessary evil.

Two days before my transplant, a nurse came in to speak with Bob and me about the protocol of my isolation period. I had just assumed I would be "locked up" and that would be that, but things are never that simple when so much is at stake. The nurse had a checklist about five pages long which detailed all of the dos and don'ts. Wearing a mask and disinfecting one's hands prior to coming into my room was only the beginning of what rules had to be followed. I could never have imagined what full isolation really meant…probably a godsend in disguise. Some of the key things were as follows:

- I had to put on rubber gloves when I went to the bathroom because I could not risk getting an infection from the bacteria in my own urine or stool. That surprised me!
- If I dropped anything on the floor, I was not allowed to get it myself and had to buzz a nurse so that she could pick it up and disinfect the item before handing it back to me.
- I was instructed to keep impeccable oral hygiene as well as washing daily no matter how tired or sick I was.
- I was not allowed to leave the room other than to shower in the bathroom allocated to me across the hall. The mask had to be on and there was to be no dallying!
- Only healthy people were allowed to visit, although Bob and I had already decided that we would not encourage any visitors.
- Once daily, I would be detached from all of my lines and allowed to go shower, during which time two people would come in and change the sheets and disinfect the room from top to bottom.

- The day prior to my transplant (Thursday), I would be moved from my room to another room for a few hours. A team of cleaners would "sanitize" my room and all of my personal effects. When that was done, I would go back to my room and then I would be considered in isolation and the above six points would commence.
- For the duration of my stay in isolation, the nurses would do an even more detailed vitals check every 2-3 hours, 24/7. They would weigh me, check my blood pressure, check my mouth for any sores, listen to my breathing to make sure I did not have pneumonia, check the level of oxygen in my blood, and examine my ears and eyes. They would be watching for any abnormalities relating to the possible onset of graft-versus-host-disease or any complications due to all the drugs. The whole thing would take about 5-8 minutes. There was no worry of me feeling neglected here and certainly no chance of sleeping.

Those were the highlights of my isolation. Some of it seemed rather extreme at the time, like the wearing of rubber gloves when going to the bathroom…but, I am alive and well today so the rules are there for a reason.

On Thursday morning, Bob left and shortly thereafter I was given the results of that day's blood tests indicating that my white cell count had hit the sought after magic number "ZERO." I had undergone five days of chemotherapy, survived so far with no complications to my organs and everything would progress as laid out in the schedule we had been given. There was no turning back now.

This was the day when I was scheduled to leave my room for a few hours while it was being disinfected in preparation for my isolation time. Around mid-morning, I started to feel some very familiar cramping which only meant one thing…my damned menstrual period. How was it possible that I hadn't had my period in six months and now of all times, it showed up? In my soul I had known that this was going to happen, Murphy's Law of course, and had I not been so debilitated from the onslaught of chemo, I probably would have started throwing basins and bedpans around out of sheer rage. Why was yet one more potentially fatal complication happening to me? With a non-existent platelet count, how would they stop the bleeding? I was petrified.

When I buzzed my nurse and told her about the onset of the cramping, she said that we would play it by ear depending on how heavy my period became if it in fact arrived at all. I knew my body from 35 years of experience and it was only a matter of time…it would show up, it was just a question of how many hours from now. The bleeding was of great concern to me but I also knew that once the cramping started, there were two possible scenarios. One: I would eventually throw up from the severe pain…something that I had endured my whole life; and two: the throwing up was usually followed by passing out. It was rare that my period did not follow this pattern and I prepared myself for the worst.

Around 11:00 a.m., I was moved to a different room which had a shared bathroom with another patient next door. These rooms were obviously not for isolated patients but for people with immune systems that functioned fairly normally. I tried not to worry at the prospect of sharing a bathroom with another individual, but I knew at some point I had to face the music since I had to "go" every 15 minutes because of all the fluids I was receiving. Upon my first visit to the bathroom, I discovered that whoever was in the other room had some major health issues because drops of blood were splattered on the floor. As badly as I had to go, I turned around and waddled back to my bed, because I was not about to endanger myself by being near or coming in contact with someone else's bodily fluids. I rang for my nurse again and after she looked in the bathroom herself, arranged for a portable toilet to be brought in to me.

As I knew it would be, the severity of my cramps was escalating and I was heading towards the point of no return. While I was fretting over this, lunch arrived and true to her word, the dietician's arranged meal of raw vegetables, dip, crackers and cheese was sitting on the tray. Even though I didn't feel like eating, I knew I had to make the effort since she had gone to so much trouble. I managed to eat most of the meal and was quite proud of myself knowing that Bob would be very happy that I had actually eaten something.

About 45 minutes later, the intense pain of my cramps was bringing on increased nausea and I quickly buzzed my nurse because there wasn't any Blue Ware in sight. No sooner had I called for her, that I knew I couldn't wait for a basin to arrive. Panic stricken, I looked around the room and grabbed my large, empty water cup sitting next to my bed and promptly threw up filling it to the brim. Just as I was finishing, my nurse entered and apologized for not being there in time. She helped me clean up and gave me another bowl in case it happened again. This was the first time I had eaten in days and to no avail…I felt terribly depressed both from "losing the food" and the prospect of dealing with my period at such an inopportune time.

Within a few minutes, Bob arrived and found me in my temporary room. As soon as he walked through the door and sat on my bed, I began sobbing uncontrollably. While he held me in his arms, I told him that I had made such an effort to eat and because of the menstrual pains I had vomited. He stroked my head and tried to console me saying that he knew I had tried and that was all that mattered. I cried for a quite a while…one of the few times out of complete desperation for all of the rotten things that were happening to me. Once I calmed down, we discussed the fact that my period had arrived and, needless to say, Bob was as concerned as I because he understood the full impact of the bleeding. The last thing we wanted was for me to have additional blood transfusions and risk developing more antibodies that would put the engraftment at risk. That would be a death sentence for me.

By late afternoon, my room was disinfected and I was allowed to move back in. This marked the official beginning of my isolation and now, everyone, including Bob, had to wear a mask when they entered my room. It also meant that Bob would no longer be allowed to stay overnight. In a way, I was relieved about that because between my discomfort and the non-stop hospital interruptions Bob was not getting any sleep making it more and more difficult for him to focus on his outside responsibilities. At least now his nights at home would be more restful…he probably would not sleep that well but at least the downtime would be good for his psyche. Also, I would feel more relaxed knowing that if I wanted to get up or throw up or go to the bathroom, I wouldn't have to worry about disturbing him and waking him up. Bob stayed until about 8:00 o'clock that evening and then it was time for him to leave. We felt strange at the prospect of being separated overnight for many weeks and our parting embrace reflected that. Tomorrow was "Day 0."

For various reasons, namely pain, nausea, vomiting, and worrying over the arrival of my period, sleep eluded me once again. My menstrual flow was not out of control at this point but that was the norm since it always started slowly…would I be lucky enough that it would not escalate?

Chapter 10
October 7th to October 9th

Friday morning dawned and regardless of how exhausted I felt, I was in a positive frame of mind knowing that this was the big day! Pat and Linda would be arriving at the hospital around noon and then Pat would be prepped for the operation. Bob returned to the hospital at lunchtime so that he could meet up with Pat and Linda and have a brief visit. Pat was to be admitted at 2:00 p.m. and under general anesthetic, the surgeon would extract the bone marrow by inserting a needle into various sites in the hipbone. Once the marrow was harvested, it would be "processed" and the fluid would be bagged and brought to my room. Under the supervision of my lead nurse, Pat's marrow would be infused (just like a blood or platelet transfusion) and I would be monitored for any signs of possible distress such as seizures, heart attack, drop in blood pressure, etc. When people ask me nowadays whether the actual transplant was painful, I am reluctant to answer that it is "only" a transfusion because it gives a completely incorrect impression. It is not that the transplant itself is painful; it is what you must endure physically in order to be prepared for it…that is the dangerous part about a bone marrow transplant.

By 3:30 p.m., we were told that everything had gone according to plan and there were no complications. Pat confessed later that he had been scared to death! He, like me, had never had any health issues and he nearly fainted when his IV was inserted. When he was asked to walk to another room with the IV in, his knees began to buckle and he didn't think he would make it to his destination. In total, the doctors had extracted two liters of bone marrow from Pat…he was a skinny guy and I couldn't believe he had that much in him. The requirement for the quantity of bone marrow needed was based on the weight of the recipient and I'm sure that Pat was grateful that I didn't weight 300 pounds! He commented weeks afterward that if I had a problem engrafting, it had better be sooner than later because then the surgeons would be able to reuse the existing entry points in his hips…we had a good chuckle when he said that.

At 5:30 p.m. my lead nurse came in with my "life" in two bags. After making sure that these bags were indeed meant for me (everyone always double- and triple-checked the information on blood products and most especially something as vital as bone marrow), they were attached to the tree and hooked up to one of my catheter lines. The appearance of the marrow was not dissimilar to platelets only slightly more pinkish in color. When the infusion started, I began to think about the imagery that my friend had sent me regarding the raging fire and now I focused on the "life-sustaining rain" as it entered my veins. Bob and I barely spoke. Even though the procedure appeared simple, a serious side effect on my part could prove fatal both from the standpoint of the reaction itself and the fact that if I reacted, there could be no transplant and that meant…

My lead nurse stayed for over an hour, frequently taking my blood pressure and checking my breathing. When it seemed that I was coping well with the incoming bone marrow, she left us for a little while. Within a few minutes, another nurse stopped by to say that Pat had woken up from the anesthetic and he was being wheeled to our floor so that I could see him through my window. Typically, the curtains were always drawn across windows that faced into the hallway of the ward, but on this occasion, we opened them. It was a poignant moment when Pat and Linda looked through the glass and saw me being infused with Pat's marrow. Pat looked completely spent and by the color of him, I had the feeling that I wasn't the only one who was dealing with nausea. Now it was time for Bob to leave. He had arranged to drive Pat and Linda back to our home to spend the night so that they could return to the hospital the following day and have Pat's dressings changed. Pat was sick several times during the drive to our house...luckily Bob had anticipated this and brought a container for him to throw up in. Throughout the evening, Pat continued to be sick while Bob and Linda ate a dinner of roasted chicken and potato salad that a dear friend had supplied. Even if Pat didn't feel like celebrating, they were!

The entire infusion of marrow took about three hours and it was nearly 10:00 p.m. by the time the transplant was finished. Even though I had no serious complications, my body felt exceptionally strange. Each time I lay down, within two minutes I would have the sensation that my bed was vibrating. At first I thought there was actually an earthquake or there was something going on in the building that was causing it to shake, but then I realized it was all internal. Not being able to deal with the unsettling feeling, I'd get out of bed and stand in the middle of my room hoping that whatever it was would go away. That, along with the discomfort of the Hickman in my body, made slumber impossible. If I thought I had been tired before, this was the Mount Everest of overtiredness. I spent the entire night getting in and out of bed every fifteen minutes, sometimes standing, sometimes sitting in a chair. In the darkness of my room, with only the light of the sensors and gauges, I wept because I could not SLEEP wondering whether I would ever sleep again. This was not what I had envisioned as my post-transplant night, which perhaps made it seem all the worse...somehow I had imagined it more joyful. Bone marrow transplant experts say the transplant itself is anticlimactic…I can vouch for that.

By daybreak, the tingling sensations had stopped and I was back to feeling "normal;" whatever that was. Bob arrived late morning and told me that Pat was doing well, other than being sore, and they were on their way home. Now began the critical part – the wait and see game until engraftment. Just because I had been lucky enough to have a match did not mean that I would engraft but that possibility was not discussed, only thought. The unwavering optimism of the doctors and nurses was reflected in a betting pool that was held for each transplant patient. Anyone was welcome to join in and a calendar for the month of October had been tacked to my bulletin board where people would fill in their names on the date they thought I would show my first white cell count. Doctors and nurses alike participated. My white cell count was currently zero so even a 0.1 would be an indicator that something was happening. Bob and I also joined the pool with Bob choosing October 18th and I more conservatively picking October 22nd…I didn't want to be disappointed by being too confident.

As was standard procedure for a transplant patient, we were given a brochure from the Medic-Alert society so that we could order and receive a bracelet prior to my leaving the hospital. The purpose of the bracelet was for any medical personnel, in the event of an accident, to know that I was a bone marrow transplant patient and that if I needed a blood transfusion, the blood product had to have all white cells removed…or irradiated as it was called. If I was transfused with non-irradiated blood, it was possible that my new marrow could reject. I thought it was amazing that they would get us to order a bracelet when we didn't even know if I would engraft or survive, but such was their optimism for their patients. Bob filled out the form and ordered me a gold bracelet even though there were cheaper ones available saying that he had no doubts I would make it and that

I deserved the gold one. It wasn't that I was being pessimistic, but I had always been a super-practical person and I thought what a waste of money it would be to get the gold one if I wasn't around to wear it. You can't change who you are even in those situations.

The highlight of my first transplanted day was that I was able and in the mood to start emailing family and friends. There was no wireless internet access available in 3Z, which gave Bob a bit of a challenge as to how to get me connected but using the dial up modem in my laptop, a long phone cable, and a phone card, he had me set up in no time. The only tricky thing was that the phone jack was on the other side of the room and I had to drag my tree and lines each time I wanted to use the computer which meant being especially careful not to get a line hooked on anything for fear of pulling it out my chest. If that happened, a new Hickman would have to be inserted and we didn't want to go there.

I sent a mass email to everyone detailing my transplant of the previous day, giving them a small insight as to what had happened during my week of chemotherapy. It became part of my routine to check my emails each morning – and at night, when my surroundings were quieter and I was feeling more alone, I would answer the dozens of emails I received daily. My transplant saga acquired a momentum of its own and through friends of friends of friends, I soon heard from people that I had not communicated with in 20-30 years. When I answered my emails it was as if each of these people were sitting in my room and it made the isolation less lonely. Every few days I would write a mass email if something particularly interesting or funny or awkward happened and usually everyone responded whether it was only with a few words or several paragraphs.

The emailing sometimes helped to take my mind off the nausea, but overall it was still a big problem and I had barely eaten in days. I was receiving two types of antinausea medication and each one could only be administered for 6 hours at a time due to their side effects and potency which left 12 hours of my day with nothing to control the nausea. Bob and I discussed this with my nurses and after a team meeting, it was decided that the timing of the antinausea meds needed to be tweaked so that I would receive them shortly before my meals. Hopefully, that would give me enough time to eat and keep everything down. One thing I cannot stress enough is that you, as a patient, should be involved in your care. I soon learned what the schedule was for each drug that I received and on the odd occasion when there were mix-ups (nurses and doctors are only human), I was able to catch them because I was aware of what I should be receiving. Another example was the fluconazole that I was on. I was to take four pills each morning and I realized quickly that within an hour of taking these pills, I would throw up. Obviously, my system was not able to handle that many at once. I consulted one of the hematologists and asked if I could take two in the morning and two at night. Once that was changed, I had no vomiting – at least not from the fluconazole.

Within a couple of days of rearranging the schedule of my antinausea medication, I was able to eat a bit without my meal coming back. The meal that I looked forward to the most, was the one of raw vegetables with ranch dressing because the meal was cold and there was no aroma to upset my stomach. I loved the crunch of the vegetables and let's face it, you could put ranch dressing on socks and they would taste excellent! The problem was that more often than not, my special meal did not arrive and in its place would be something like a plate with wilted lettuce, canned pears and cottage cheese and I felt the same way about cottage cheese as I did Jell-O. Each time I received one of these disgusting dinners, I left it untouched which caused raised eyebrows from the nurses who kept track of such things.

By day three of the onset of my period, Dr. Wasi and her team decided to put me on the pill because the flow kept increasing and they were worried about my blood loss. They too, did not want me to have any more blood transfusions than absolutely necessary. As expected, the pill stopped my period within a few days and we all breathed a sigh of relief feeling that we were out of the woods …or so we thought.

Sunday, October 9th was the day before Thanksgiving and Bob spent most of that day with me before leaving for home in the late afternoon. Much to his surprise and delight, a complete Thanksgiving dinner with all the trimmings as well as instructions, awaited him in our refrigerator. The Thanksgiving fairy had dropped by! As he was opening all of the containers, the doorbell rang and it was Mike delivering yet another full turkey meal courtesy of his wife and family. Bob immediately phoned the hospital and told me what these thoughtful friends had done and how much he appreciated a home cooked meal…turkey dinner was his absolute favorite to boot. I was thrilled to hear this because I had been quite upset at the thought of him being alone on Thanksgiving with only a freezer meal to thaw. Many people offered their help while I was hospitalized but Bob mostly refused it because he was (and is) so fiercely independent. The truly thoughtful friends and acquaintances completely ignored him and helped regardless of his baulking and we are so very thankful to them all.

Knowing that Bob was looked after and about to enjoy a sumptuous Thanksgiving dinner, and the fact that this was the first day I had not thrown up, I was actually looking forward to the arrival of my own meal. Visions of ranch dressing danced in my head! At 5:00 p.m. my meal tray arrived and I could have cried as I stared at a rubber cheese sandwich on white mushy bread...not even a pickle or salad on the side. I was devastated which seems rather silly, but when you are locked in a room and are totally reliant on other people to provide you with the necessities, every little thing becomes a big thing. My meal was a BIG THING to me especially now that I had an appetite of sorts. I kept thinking about Bob and his two holiday dinners and here I was a prisoner, alone in a cell with a cheese sandwich for supper. All I could think of was all the families that were having a festive evening with a luscious meal…and then there was me…I felt very sorry for myself. I pressed the buzzer for my nurse…long gone were the days of feeling guilty over calling them…I had no choice…they were *it*!

When I explained why I was so upset, my nurse bent over backwards to accommodate me. She went to the little kitchen in 3Z that was for the use of the patients and their families and it contained a refrigerator, microwave and toaster. It didn't have much in the way of food and the most innovative my nurse could be was toasting some bread and topping it with jam. On her way back to my room, she raided another patient's untouched food tray and procured a small salad and cup of yoghurt. It was no feast but it was better than what I had started with. Happy Thanksgiving, I thought.

Chapter 11
October 10th to October 14th

On October 10th, having about eleven days under my belt in the hospital, I sent out a mass email detailing what my daily life was like in isolation. It is unedited and copied from my email folder:

Hello Everyone,
I know that some of you may be wondering what my life is like these days...since things are fairly stable right now I thought I would give you a time by time schedule of my 24 hour days. Hope you find it somewhat interesting...if not, just use it to light a fire...HA HA!

6:00 a.m.   Wake up call...not quite like at the Ritz though. Daily bloodtaking at this time of about 4 vials out of the hickman inserted in my chest. Sort of like tapping a maple syrup tree only it's for blood! Then the vitals check...weigh in/nice cold stethoscope on my chest & back to check my breathing... hopefully I'm still alive (HA HA). Then, blood pressure check, oxygen check, and temperature check. It's sort of like being at a really nice spa without the special trimmings. Yeah right!
6:15 a.m.   Free time to sleep until 8:00 a.m.
7:00 a.m.   More antinausea meds through the IV before breakfast time so I don't bring the whole thing back!
8:00 a.m.   Breakfast...cheerios/milk/muffin and yoghurt. All low fat...which I really need...NOT! There is no choice...I guess there are a lot of fat people out there so there is no choice. Call from Bob to say good morning...that's the best part!

9:00 a.m.   I usually check my emails at this time.

9:30 a.m.   I get capped off (they undo my lines from the IV pole) so I can go and shower in a room across the hall which is sterilized and kept only for my use. My room does not have a shower so at first that bummed me out. Now, I look forward to that 10 step walk to the shower to see my only glimpse of the day of the outside world. I must wear a mask when I go outside and anyone that comes into my room must wear one also and wash their hands.

10:00 a.m.   A complete vitals check again as at 6:00 a.m.

10:30 a.m.   One hour of freedom in my room without being tied to the IV pole. I can do jumping jacks, jump on the bed, do head flips etc, etc...yeah right!

11:00 a.m.   Time for the dressing change on my hickman surgery. This is done daily right after I shower so that the bandages come off easier. Hopefully, when it heals better in a few days that will only need to be done every three days.

11:15 a.m.   I'm hooked back to the IV pole and more meds are hung for antinausea, antibiotics and other various things.

12:00 p.m.   Lunch

12:30 p.m.   Try and get a nap in...contrary to popular belief...you do not get to rest in a hospital.

1:30 p.m.   Bob just brought me my guitar so I think I'll try and play a little at this time.

2:00 p.m.   Another vitals check

2:30 p.m.   Visit from Bob give or take one hour one way or another. We usually chat and play scrabble. I tell him about all the interesting emails I got and he tells me what is going on at home, etc. Let me take this time to say that Bob is a saint. What that man has done is incredible! Talk about someone rising to the very difficult job of being a caregiver. One of the hardest jobs in the world.

3:00 p.m.   Hang more medication for anti nausea or whatever.

4:30 p.m.   Bob usually stays about 3 hours or so. The poor guy has to sit here the entire time with a mask on that must be changed every hour or so it does not saturate with germs.

5:00 p.m.   Gourmet dinner...yeah right!

6:00 p.m.   I maybe watch movie on my laptop or something on T.V. Another vitals check.

7:00 p.m.   Start answering my emails that I received in the morning. I keep them and send them in the morning for when I go on line!

8:00 p.m.   More stuff is hung on the IV plus meds to take orally. I forgot to mention that happens also about 5 times per day.

9:00 p.m.   Get into bed and watch some t.v. till about 10:00 p.m.

10:00 p.m.   Another vitals check.

11:00 p.m.   Kiss good night...only kidding...just checking to see if you were paying attention!!!!

2:00 a.m.   Vitals check again. That cold stethoscope feels reeaaaallllly good at 2:00 a.m. in the morning out of a dead sleep.

6:00 a.m.   Starts all over again!

So folks, there you have it. An exciting day in the life of Esther Hougham. Hey, you think I'm kidding about excited. I'm excited because I feel pretty good and don't have worse mouth sores yet and still have my hair...although those are still subject to change!

Take care all and if I have anything to say is to enjoy your day... regardless of what it brings...it's the only one we've got!

Love

Esther

As I reread this particular email, I am reminded that I had asked Bob to bring my guitar to the hospital. He was thrilled at the prospect of me playing because he felt that it was a small step towards me being normal again and that perhaps our life would be what it had once been. I tried to play a few times but my fingers were so weak that it was painful to play and I kept knocking my footstool over and dropping my pick on the floor. Each time that happened, I'd have to disturb the nurses from their important work and have them pick up and disinfect these items before I could handle them again. The whole thing became a frustrating ordeal and only emphasized how weak I was. Within a couple of days, I reluctantly asked Bob to take my guitar back home. He told me several months afterwards that he cried in the car because it only reinforced we were light years away from me being well again.

At night, out of boredom, I had started watching some TV but only documentaries on a health channel that featured stories about patients and how they dealt with rare and sometimes terminal illnesses. Either before or after these programs, I'd spend a couple of hours on the phone speaking to Mom and Pat and Linda. I looked forward to my conversations with Pat because he always boosted my morale and through our talks, we learned over and over again how many things we had in common. Mom on the other hand could not keep the sorrow out of her voice and I would hang up worrying about the stress I was causing her. Soon Memke would be returning to Belgium and then Mom would be left alone with nothing to do but agonize over me. I wondered how she would handle that.

As each day came and went, the nurses were amazed that my health actually improved as opposed to the contrary, which was normally the case when your white cell count was "0" and you awaited engraftment. I had been at that level for five days now but I showed no signs of further deterioration, such as worsening of mouth sores, increased infections and the like. According to the printed timeline that I had been given prior to my transplant, I knew I was theoretically about to commence the nadir phase of the schedule. The proof of the pudding of how unusually well I was doing was the fact that I rarely saw Dr. Wasi. Her visits were reserved for the patients with serious complications but she did drop by for the occasional pep talk. Mostly I was examined by the many resident hematologists who were gaining experience in that teaching hospital.

Once my nausea was under control, I began to feel like my old self again other than I was still gravely ill of course! I made an effort to apply my make-up daily and wear the colorful mix-and-match pajamas that Vicki had chosen for me, all of which did help me feel less like a patient and more of a person. Surprisingly, I still had a full head of hair but I doubted that would last much longer. One of my nurses had counseled that when my hair started falling out, it would be time to give me a buzz cut otherwise my room would become too messy and unsanitary.

Chapter 12
October 15th to October 17th

That day did arrive. On the morning of October 15th, two weeks after starting the chemo, there were large clumps of hair laying on my pillow. I mentioned it to my nurse when she came in and we arranged that prior to my showering, she would bring in the clippers and shave my head. It seemed rather unceremonious but really, how else do you get rid of a lot of hair quickly? The whole process brought to mind one of Mom's WWII stories in Belgium where some of the women in her village had their heads shaved as punishment for having consorted with the invading German troops. Sometimes weird thoughts crept into my brain! Coming from good European stock, I had always had lots of hair and I nervously wondered how I would feel once I was bald.

At 10:00 a.m., my nurse came in with a huge set of clippers. I chuckled to myself since they were exactly the same size as the ones we used on the horses to sheer their coats every once in awhile. First horse serum, now horse clippers…this whole thing was getting stranger by the minute. Chan, my nurse, put a sheet on my shoulders as if I were in a hair salon…talk about an oxymoron…and asked me if I was ready? I nodded and off she went. It took her about 15 minutes to shave my head with the occasional "Ouch" coming from me because the clippers had a few teeth missing and they would catch on my scalp. She apologized and mentioned that they should really get a new pair…Uh, Huh! If I escaped alive, meaning the transplant,

I vowed to donate a new set of clippers to the ward. When she finished, Chan looked at me and pronounced that I suited being bald, explaining that not everyone was lucky enough to have a nicely shaped, small skull. Lucky is in the eye of the beholder, I guess! After she cleaned up all the hair from the floor which looked like she had shaved a yak, I was left alone to contemplate my new "look." I sat there for a while, actually afraid to look at myself in the mirror. Eventually, I gathered enough courage to grab my pole and walked to the edge of my little bathroom. Taking a deep breath, I slowly peered around the corner and stared at the face of a stranger. I, in fact, did look exactly like one of those promiscuous WWII women except I hadn't had nearly the fun! I got a hold of myself and thought...hey, I'm alive...nothing else matters. My make-up bag was lying on the edge of the sink and I slapped on the usual eyeliner, lipstick and rouge, wrapped a funky scarf around my head that Bob had brought in preparation for this day and looked at myself again. I decided I didn't look half-bad.

During the afternoon, several nurses and residents came in to see me because they had heard that my head had been shaved. A point was made of lending moral support when the patient reached this stage. They all commented on how well I looked, especially with the make-up, the scarf and coordinated pajamas and I wondered whether they were just being nice or was it fact? One of the young residents who saw me daily said that she always looked forward to seeing me because she wondered which matching outfit and scarf I would be wearing that day and, I have to say, hearing that did lift my spirits. I soon realized that I was an anomaly given what I was supposed to be going through at this stage of the game. I think it amazed them that here I was looking and acting quite healthy when I should have been in the absolute worst shape in terms of the "timeline." Maybe these 12 bags of drugs weren't as bad as I had initially thought!

When Bob arrived later that day, he expressed no shock at seeing me without my hair. He was just happy to be seeing me in any shape or form.

Below is an email I sent out to all my email friends:

Hello Everyone,

Finally a few pictures of Esther and her hamster cage. You'll notice that there is no wheel for me to exercise on yet! Who knows what next week will bring!

There is only one shot of me...probably enough anyway and a few pics (panoramic...yeah right!) of the gorgeous view of the room itself. IT has all the comforts of home without the home!

I just thought you would like to see what I look like these days sans the hair and what my environment looks like. Not quite the Pestana Palace that we stayed at in Portugal in March but I'll tell you, when I walk out of here alive and healthy it will be a better memory!

Love to you all and once again thank you for your continuing support and emails. They make me feel like I am part of the world outside!

Love Esther

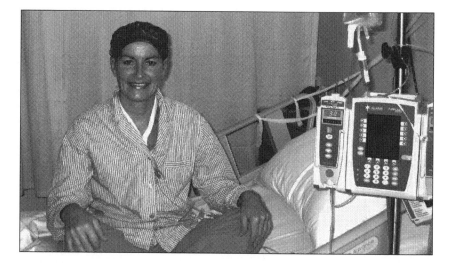

The hair loss saga did not end with my head. Two days after I was shaved, as I was showering in my segregated bathroom, I noticed another mass of hair in the drain. "Other areas" were giving up their hair too and after I finished showering I decided I wouldn't need to use a razor for months…this was the best bikini cut I had ever had! To make light of the whole matter, I sent out emails with catchy subject lines like; "Hair Today, Gone Tomorrow," and "Hairless in Seattle." The first one to jump on the "hairless" bandwagon was Pat by sending me a crazy picture of himself wearing a ridiculous Jamaican, dreadlock hat. It was hysterical! Soon, the rest of my European cousins joined in and I was receiving pictures from Belgium and Germany with all of them wearing outrageous hats. One of my Belgian cousins even sent a picture of their Weimaraner dog wearing a felt fedora. I laughed like I hadn't laughed in a long time when I saw their photos. These were the kinds of things that made my isolation endurable.

Chapter 13
October 18ᵗʰ to October 22ⁿᵈ

Within a couple of days of being shaved, I realized that I needed some headwear. You have no idea how cold your head can get (the bald people can identify) when you have no hair. The hats that the hospital provided were generously knitted by volunteers but they looked more like skullcaps and lacked any style or panache. I was sick but I wasn't dead yet! My mother's words came back to me again: "If you look good, you feel good!" If I had to wear a hat, then it at least had to be attractive…I needed all the psychological help I could get. I enlisted the shopping help of our office supervisor Vicki and she found three hats and several more scarves. She was especially clever because she knew what colors my pajamas were and tried to come up with selections that matched them. My girlfriend Leslie emailed and said she would go on a hat quest with the sole intent of finding me something smashing…she was a clothing consultant at the time so I trusted her taste implicitly. Between the two shipments, I had a hat for every occasion. It added to the fun that everyone had when they came in to see me. I think I was becoming a bit of a wonder in 3Z. When I had discussed my baldness with Janet she had pleaded with me not to get a wig. I agreed with her for the sole reason that I was proud of my baldness because it signified my fight for life. I was not ashamed and therefore would not pretend that I had hair. She joked that if she ever got sick and lost her hair, she would have to wear a cycling helmet to cover her head because she had a Neanderthal-sized skull.

Everything was moving along better than expected but Murphy's Law once again plagued us. My daily blood results had shown a significant increase in my liver enzymes and the doctors attributed the abnormality to the birth control pills that I had been on in order to stop my period. Having no choice, they took me off the pill and surprise, surprise, the flood gates opened and the nurses couldn't keep me supplied with enough sanitary napkins to keep up. (Tampons were out of the question from an infection standpoint.) For five days, I had to change pads every 35 minutes. My hemoglobin count had actually risen due to the infusion of Pat's two liters of bone marrow but now it had dwindled to less than 99. Anything below 90 meant another blood transfusion. We kept our fingers crossed that I would engraft before I reached 90 and would therefore not need another blood transfusion. My period lasted a very long, stressful week before it finally gave up…probably because there was nothing left!

With my heavy period, I had more soiled clothing than usual. Bob had been doing my laundry during my time in isolation because one of "the Rules" had been that I had to have clean clothes daily and since I wasn't wearing hospital issue, Bob was the lucky winner for that chore. He hadn't washed clothes in 29 years but by this time, he was an expert. Each day he would bring a cloth bag that held the previous day's clothes and he would take home what needed to be laundered which usually included pajamas, underwear, socks and a bathrobe. Because of my heavy menstrual bleeding, he had to deal with removing bloodstains and one of the nurses gave him a handy tip for that problem. She said that the best way to get blood out of anything was to pour hydrogen peroxide on the stain and let it fizz. Once the fizz was gone, launder as normal. It worked!

We got through each day much the same way. Bob arrived in the early to mid-afternoon and stayed for about three hours. Naturally, I looked forward to the afternoons for that very reason. Just before he came, I would position myself facing the curtain that blocked the view of my door. I learned that the only way I could identify who was walking in, was by looking under the curtain and guess at whose feet they were. I jokingly began calling Bob "Mr. Brown Shoes." Once he was coined that, he decided to only wear those shoes because then I would know that it was him.

What we did during his visits, depended on my energy level and how I felt. If it was a really good day, we would play Scrabble. Under normal circumstances, we had always been evenly matched but given the number of drugs I was on, I couldn't always think straight. The nurses thought it quite amusing that Bob cut me no slack and kicked my derriere regularly with not even an ounce of guilt. He told me he would never let me win because it would show that he felt sorry for me and he knew I wouldn't like that…maybe. Some days we had to quit playing because just having to think made me as tired as now cycling 30 miles! I had been told that chemotherapy did take a toll on some people's memory and ability to think, but over time the effects disappeared. I trusted they were right because I had always prided myself on a decent memory and this feeling of my brains being scrambled did not impress me in the least. On other occasions, if I was completely drained, Bob would just read his book in the vinyl recliner that sat near my bed and I would sleep. I'd feel guilty that he had driven an hour to see me and I couldn't even hold a decent conversation but there wasn't much I could do about it. Some days when I felt this way, he would snuggle alongside me in the bed, spoon fashion and we would both nap. I wasn't the only one who was tired. The nurses still came in for their scheduled vitals check but upon seeing us sleeping, would quietly tiptoe out of the room and return later. They did their best to empathize with what the patient and their loved ones were going through.

During one of his visits, Bob looked at me rather quizzically and asked whether I felt anything unusual in my right eye. I said that I did not. He then told me that my right eye was staring in a totally different direction than my left eye. He said…"You look like Marty Feldman!" I jumped off the bed and dragged my tree to the bathroom to see what the heck he was talking about. When I looked in the mirror, I could not see anything unusual. As long as I was looking at myself, the eye was focusing on me but when I would just be sitting there, not thinking about it, my eye would do its own thing. Bob called the nurse in and she too noticed that it was wandering. She felt that it was due to one of the antinausea medications I was receiving and they would keep an "eye" on it so to speak. The side effects from some of these drugs were creepy but my nurse did feel that the eye would go back to normal once I was off the drugs. What a lovely sight I must have been…bald with a wandering eye!

One morning, during Bob's usual phone chat with me at 8:00 a.m. or so, I asked him to stop somewhere on the way to the hospital and find me a submarine sandwich. He nearly dropped the phone in disbelief at what he was hearing. With the return of my appetite, I had developed an uncontrollable craving for a whole-wheat sub, laden with lettuce, hot peppers, tomato, cheese, mayonnaise and mustard. I never even ate that in my "B.I." (before illness) life and I had no idea where that came from. Bob wrote down my request because he knew he wouldn't be able to remember all of those ingredients and said that he knew of a submarine shop that was very near the hospital. When he arrived for his visit that afternoon, I nearly tackled him, pole-in-tow! I sat cross-legged on the bed and devoured that sub as if I had never eaten anything as delicious in my entire life. Bob sat on the recliner, smiling the whole time as he watched me eat. I hadn't seen him that happy in weeks other than when he was beating me at Scrabble perhaps…

The submarine became the admittance ticket for every visit… as a matter of fact, Bob was not allowed to enter my room unless he had it in hand…only kidding but that was how I felt. I loved them so much that by the third day we increased the quantity to two because Bob would stash the second sub in the ward kitchen and my nurse brought it to me at supper time. At least now with my ace in the hole sandwich, I didn't have to worry anymore about whether the hospital cafeteria served me something that I would and could eat. There wasn't much excitement in my life as I previously said, everything within those four walls became a big thing…including that sub. I laughed when Bob commented that the only reason I wanted to see him was because he was the submarine delivery guy. A couple of days after I started eating the sandwiches, the news spread around the ward and no one could believe that a bone marrow transplant patient at this stage was devouring two submarines per day. Most patients of my tenure were either still throwing up or they had feeding tubes because their mouths were so sore that they could not eat in the conventional manner. I was becoming a bit of a miracle story in the ward. I have to say though, that most of the patients in 3Z had leukemia and not only did they receive chemotherapy prior to the transplant but also full body radiation. That took more of a toll on them than "only" chemotherapy.

Now that I was hungry again, I figured out how to play with the hospital menus. It wasn't that I could eat everything…"Ensure" and hot meals were still taboo and made me feel sick, but overall, the cold foods I could eat. When I made my menu selections for the following day, termed loosely as far as "menu" goes, I tried to plan ahead. If bananas were one of the choices for instance, I would order two in a day so that I could stash one in my cupboard and save it for a special occasion. Then, when my breakfast included a bagel with peanut butter, I could haul out the banana and mush it on the bagel.

Life is reduced to the basics sometimes and this was one of those instances. Bob's grocery list for the hospital now included potato chips and ginger ale which I also added to my "treasure chest." I had been told to be careful about the potato chips because their sharp, hard edges could cut my mouth and I didn't need any more venues for infections. Each chip had to be eaten slowly and painstakingly but it was worth it! The ginger ale replaced water as my drink of choice which was strange because I had always disliked it and now, it was all I could drink. I had to consume gallons of it because the ever watchful nurses kept track of how much I drank and if they didn't see the empty cans sitting there, I got a pleasant earful about keeping up my fluid intake. As well, the ginger ale made a protein powder more palatable that I had to consume three times per day that helped keep your mouth tissue healthy and free from further deterioration. It would bubble up like an ice cream float when I mixed the pop and powder…too bad it didn't taste like it.

On the home front, Bob was developing his own routine. Because I was in the hospital and he did not have to look after me all day and night, Bob now had a bit more time to do the things he had not been able to do such as ride our horses. One horse in particular needed some extra TLC and that was CC, the ex-race horse. For the past three years I had put my heart and soul into gaining his trust both by riding him and working with him on the ground. I had used several techniques that "horse whisperers" use and invented some myself with positive results, but I knew that all of the training had to be reinforced or CC would regress. Bob and I discussed this and even though he had rarely ridden CC, we decided that the time was right for Bob to continue where I had left off. It was a challenge for Bob because riding CC was like walking on eggshells….Bob had to tread lightly for fear of undoing my work. When Bob came for his afternoon visits, he would explain in detail how that day's ride had gone and I felt as if I had ridden him myself. Horses do not accept just anyone, especially if they have been abused at some point in their lives, and I was delighted that CC allowed Bob to get on him. These were the types of discussions we used to have during cocktail hour (B.I.) talking endlessly about horses, our training philosophies, and what had worked that day or not. This was a welcome distraction from the constant barrage of gloom and doom.

Another diversion for Bob was the occasional visit from some of his guy friends. They would invite themselves over for the night and bring all the fixings for dinner with Bob only having to provide a BBQ and perhaps a side dish. It was amusing because Bob would ask mc during his afternoons at the hospital what he should make and I would suggest various choices as he carefully wrote down my instructions. I always found it such a role reversal. He told me that he loved it when people came to visit but he didn't like the extra work of stripping the beds and cleaning bathrooms afterwards, which I thought quite funny because I had been telling him that for years and now he finally understood. When he commented on the work involved, I would nod in agreement and give that Cheshire cat smile. Sometimes, good things come out of bad and gaining a greater understanding of my "jobs" was one of them.

The day following one of these "guy" evenings, Bob had asked his two buddies to drop off some potato chips at the hospital since they would be driving by anyway on their way home. I had reached the critical "crumbs at the bottom of the bag" stage and had sent out an SOS via phone for more chips. Jim and Brad decided they would leave the bags at the nurses' station because they knew I couldn't have any visitors. The most they hoped for was that I would pull my curtains back and give them a wave through the window. When they arrived, my lead nurse Leah made an executive decision and before they knew what hit them, they were ushered in with masks on. Talk about a couple of reluctant dragons…it's not that they didn't want to see me, but they worried that they would somehow infect me with something and endanger my life. They stood as close to the entry as possible, shifting from one leg to the other not really knowing what to say which was totally understandable. Things like "how are you doing" or "what have you been up to" seemed just a trifle frivolous but they did comment that I looked better than what they had expected. I took that as a compliment. As Jim was talking, I glanced at Brad and saw tears welling in his eyes. I'll never forget that. After they left, I felt depressed because seeing these two dear, long time friends only reinforced how lonely I was and how much I missed everybody.

One of the rituals that Bob and I developed when he came to visit was the reading of every email that I received daily in addition to the get-well cards that he brought from home. I would read them all while sitting on the bed and savor each one as if it were a fine Belgian chocolate. A very good friend, Owen, made it his mission to mail a card at least every two to three days. What was particularly appreciated about this was that at the time of my "incarceration" he was vacationing in India and he even continued the mailing from the other side of the world. Judging by the quantity I had received so far, I was convinced that he must have taken an entire suitcase of get-well cards with him because from the content and style, he had certainly not purchased them in India. Equally entertaining, in addition to his cards, were the incredibly humorous travel journals that he wrote and emailed every couple of days to a select group of friends and acquaintances. We had told him on many occasions that he should have picked writing as a profession instead of the more boring retail establishment that he owned. When I received the very first journal of this particular trip to India, I was touched beyond words to read that he dedicated his musings to me and to what Bob and I were facing. Weeks after I was discharged, I was still receiving cards that Owen had sent from India...to this day they sit in a drawer and every once in a while I pull them out and have a good laugh...and a tear.

All of my cards, as well as pictures that I printed from emails were pinned to the bulletin board in my room which now resembled communication central complete with laptop, printer, camera, iPod and various USB cables. I think the nurses, as well as the cleaning staff, were just a wee bit frustrated at times trying to deal with moving around my room but, hey, I needed something to stay sane and all of that kept my mind occupied. I know I could not have survived those weeks in my hamster cage had it not been for staying in touch whether it was by email or phone.

With each day that passed, a large X was marked off on the calendar. Soon we would be reaching the first day chosen for my engraftment as part of the "pool" and we tried not to get too anxious about if and when that might happen. We reminded ourselves that a full transplant typically took longer than other types of bone marrow transplants. For instance, in advanced leukemia patients, a more expedient transplant was performed wherein only stem cells were used for the transplant as opposed to the full blood product as had been the case with me. The stem cell transplant could be likened to laying down sod as opposed to sowing seeds and waiting for them to grow which I now awaited. You got more "bang for your buck" with the pure stem cells but the preferred method for me had been the traditional full transplant. The interesting thing about the stem cell extraction was that they would give the donor a drug that increased the production of the stem cells...sort of like putting fertilizer on grass. After about five days of being supercharged, the donor would actually begin to feel heavy and "fat" due to the increased production. Once the doctors felt that there was enough to harvest, the donor would get a reverse blood transfusion which was processed through a special machine that siphoned out the stem cells. I know there is much controversy regarding stem cells and stem cell research but when you are on my side of the fence, need I say, I can see only its benefits. The whole process of a transplant, whichever type, is miraculous.

Today was October 19th and I had passed the targeted date that Bob had selected for my engraftment. When I received my blood results that morning from my daily tests, I was surprised to see that my platelet count had barely fallen from the previous day's number, which was highly unusual given that typically they depleted at a rate of about 8,000 to 12,000 daily. I had become an expert at my counts and I knew exactly what the lifespan and correct levels were for hemoglobin, platelets and white cells. Curiously I looked at my white cell count but it was still at "0." No engraftment of white cells but strange that my platelets had stayed virtually status quo. I mentioned this oddity to my nurse and she informed me that white cells were always the first to engraft and the fact that my platelets had stayed the same meant nothing. I'm no doctor, but I knew how my body had functioned these past six weeks and THIS platelet inconsistency had never happened before; I disagreed but said nothing. When I explained my counts to Bob that morning during our customary 8:00 a.m. phone conversation, he agreed that it did not follow the normal pattern and perhaps we did have reason to be cautiously optimistic.

That night I went to bed and fell into a rare, deep sleep only to be awoken by an intense hot flash accompanied with an overwhelming feeling of claustrophobia. I jumped up in bed gasping for air feeling like I was being cooked from the inside out. My first thought was, "Why am I having a hot flash?" I hadn't been plagued by one since late June, before I started taking the Black Cohosh. When my hot flashes had initially started, and especially when they occurred during the night, I'd have to run outside and let the evening air cool me off and only then, could I return to bed. What would I do now? There was nowhere for me to go! It took every ounce of self-control I had not to tear out my IVs, run to the elevator and escape to the street below – and freedom. I reluctantly rang for my night nurse. Jane quickly sorted out that I was having a major crisis and came up with a compromise, since allowing me to leave the building was not an option. She suggested that if it made me feel less contained, I could sit just outside my door in the hallway for a short while as long as I put a mask on. Once I knew that I could actually leave my room, the powerful urge to get away ceased. Jane also recommended drawing back the curtains covering the large window that looked onto the ward hallway assuming that it would help me feel less claustrophobic. With that open, I could see the nurses walking back and forth and the general goings on of the ward; it reminded me of sitting at a sidewalk café watching the world go by…minus the chardonnay and ambiance. After Jane left, I sat cross-legged on my bed and spent time staring out the window and I was surprised at the activity going on around me. At first I thought I would feel too obvious sitting there with everyone able to look in at me, but I was just happy to see something other than my four walls and its contents. THAT was getting very old! A female patient about my age looked up as she walked past my window and we exchanged shy smiles. Judging by the direction she was going, I guessed she occupied the room next door and was the person I heard throwing up during my first week of chemo. Jane told me later that this patient, Nancy, had received her transplant the day before mine and we were more or less on the same recovery schedule although she appeared quite ragged to me. I also learned that she had suffered from Acute Myeloid Leukemia, hence the transplant, and had required full body radiation in addition to the chemo...no wonder she didn't look too spry. Feeling a bit more in control of myself now, I settled back into bed leaving the curtains open for the night.

When my morning blood results arrived the next day, I was disappointed to see that my white cells had remained at a big fat ZERO; however, my platelets showed a small increase from the previous day. I didn't bother making any comments to my nurse since once again, no one thought this extraordinary but I did tell Bob during our morning conversation. We were beginning to feel very excited about my platelets, but decided not to say anything to family and friends for fear of giving them false hope. This was our "little secret" for now. I also told Bob about my hot flashes during the night and we wondered whether it was because I was becoming healthy again...translation... I was engrafting!

Later in the afternoon, Bob arrived bearing two sets of needlepoint that he had asked Angela (the same good friend who had supplied the roast chicken and potatoes for Bob, Linda and Pat on transplant night) to choose and purchase for him. He felt that if I had something to focus on, it would keep my mind off the ever increasing claustrophobia. I had done much needlepoint in my younger days and I looked forward to working on that again…especially now that I had nothing else to do. Reading was not an option because that required concentration and the effects of the chemo made that impossible.

After Bob left, I had my usual submarine for dinner that had been stored in the fridge. I always looked forward to it but this particular one was going to taste extra special and it wasn't because of the generous dollops of mustard and mayo! When Bob had picked up my subs that day, he mentioned to the lady who always prepared them that he felt sure that I would soon be discharged. She had learned of my plight through Bob's frequent visits and she was so pleased for him that she gave him the subs "on the house." It never ceased to amaze me how many thoughtful and caring people there were in this world. Many of our friends demonstrated their concern by sending baked goods, books, even a set of Mickey Mouse pajamas. One good friend even made a cuddly afghan for my hospital bed which kept me warm on many a cold night. We were extremely lucky and appreciated all their acts of kindness.

During my regular two-hour checkup that evening, I questioned my nurse further about Nancy, the patient next door. Nurses were not in the habit of sharing personal information about other patients but she did give me a few details, one of which was that Nancy and I were indeed the same age. No wonder I felt a kinship towards her. My nurse did relay that Nancy had seen me through the window that day and had jokingly commented that it annoyed her that I had the energy and will to put on make-up while it was all she could do to get out of bed. In reality, any transplant patient was glad if another patient was doing well because it gave them hope that they would eventually follow the same path. The nurse did offer that Nancy had ended up with a feeding tube because the radiation had taken its toll on her mouth…no wonder she hadn't looked well. Thankfully, I had been spared that and if there was anything good to be said about having aplastic anemia, it was that you did not need to be radiated prior to the transplant. After my nurse left, Bob phoned for his usual "cocktail hour" conversation. Nightly, we'd spend about an hour on the phone while he sat in our family room drinking a glass of chardonnay with the fireplace lit and the dogs lying nearby. Bob placed the phone on speaker mode and set it on the coffee table so that he could hear my voice loud and clear…the only thing that was missing was me sitting on the couch next to him. The nurses thought it funny because Bob would have been visiting that afternoon and he would no sooner be home for an hour that he would call. I'm sure they could not figure out what we could possibly have left to talk about since we had just spent several hours together. That was one of the joys of our marriage…we always had something to discuss. Sadly, many evenings after we hung up, Bob wept, agonizing about whether I would ever come home. He certainly put up a good front for me.

Chapter 14

October 23rd to October 28th

The morning of October 23rd began as had all the rest since my admittance on September 29th. My blood vials were processed and shortly after breakfast, my door swung wide open and with great flourish Leah and another nurse rushed in holding a sheet of paper with my results. Leah looked at me and announced happily, "You are on your way, girl!" I didn't really understand what she meant and the look on my face must have reflected that because she explained that my white count was 0.2 that morning and where there was a 0.2 there would be a 0.3 and so on! We all began crying and hugging and talking a mile a minute. Leah said that from now on, my door could officially be kept open because I was engrafting and all I could think of was HALLELUJAH…goodbye claustrophobia! As soon as they left, I called Bob and told him that the moment we had all been waiting for had at long last arrived. He was choked up from emotion and said that he would be in as soon as he phoned my Mom and Pat and Linda to give them the exciting news. Later on that evening when I was speaking with Pat he said he never doubted for a moment that I would engraft. I truly believe that it was not lip service; in his mind there was no option other than success…I guess the "golden juice" had indeed been that.

Within an hour, I was given the criteria that I had to achieve in order to be allowed to leave the hospital:
- My white cell count needed to be at least 0.5
- I had to be fever-free for 2 consecutive days

- I had to consume a minimum of 500 calories daily
- All my meds had to be converted from IV to oral without complications

Points 2 and 3 were not an issue since I had not had a fever for over two weeks and I was eating at least 1200 calories a day thanks to the subs that Bob brought me daily. The conversion of the IV drugs to oral medications would begin immediately and I would be monitored for any adverse side effects from the switch. I was informed that the body metabolizes oral drugs differently than by way of IV and there would probably be some upping or lowering of different medications depending on how I reacted to the changes. Therefore, now all we needed was for my white cells to reach 0.5 and it would be "Adios" hospital!

The morning of October 26th brought only a minute increase in white cells to 0.3. Bob and I were disappointed because we couldn't wait for me to be discharged and that was not likely to happen as long as I was less than 0.5. Not only had my white cells not come up in three days, but my red cells were decreasing and had reached the transfusion level stage. We did not want this because that could create more antibodies at this critical stage of engraftment. Bob talked to my nurses and suggested that we wait another twenty-four hours before transfusing with the hope that my hemoglobin would start to increase on its own by the following day. They agreed. As I said before, playing a part in your health care is important because on occasion the nurses and doctors are focused on the protocol when common sense should prevail. During the afternoon, my restlessness increased 10-fold no doubt due to the knowledge that leaving this place was just around the corner. Working on the needlepoint did help to keep my mind somewhat occupied but after almost a month of seeing virtually nothing other than those four walls, I was beginning to go shack wacky and could anyone really blame me! My hot flashes were happening regularly now and certainly confirmed the fact that they were occurring because I had the beginnings of a functioning bone marrow. I never thought that I would welcome being afflicted with hot flashes again but what I had endured in the past two months gave you a totally different perspective of what was annoying and what was not.

Later in the day, a resident came in to tell me that I would be receiving a white cell growth stimulator in order to speed up the development of my leukocytes because they were not increasing as quickly as expected. When Bob arrived for his visit, he was pleased that the medical team would be expediting things which meant I would be home soon! In anticipation of that, he had been given a list by the nurses of what he needed to do so that the house would be a safe environment for me. Our bungalow had to be cleaned and disinfected from one end to the other. Also, our bedding had to be washed in hot water and special pillowcases had to be purchased that would inhibit any microscopic creatures from making their way into my lungs. Those had already been bought. The bathrooms had to be free of mold and mildew and there were to be no plants or flowers in any rooms that I would frequent. We were slowly realizing that when I arrived home, I would be no different than a newborn baby leaving the hospital except that I was 48 years old and had a few more wrinkles... well maybe not! I also had the added challenges of the effects of the chemotherapy and having been taken to the edge of death.

That night was endless. A myriad of things were going through my mind and as the excitement of engrafting settled in, so with it came the worry of acquiring graft vs. host disease. As long as Pat's cells hadn't found their way into my bones, I had not dwelled on it, but now that I was engrafting, the fear became a reality. I tried to concentrate on the positive aspect of actually having a chance at a "tomorrow," but being at home without any doctors and nurses looking after me frightened the life out of me. How would I identify GVHD and how would we cope with my fragile and unpredictable recovery?

My blood results the morning of October 27th showed a whopping rise in my white cells to an amazing count of 3.2! This was well above the necessary 0.5 and if I maintained this for another day, I would be given permission to leave. At about 10:00 a.m., Leah came in all excited and said that I was to be discharged that very afternoon at two o'clock. My mouth fell open and I began stammering things like "But I haven't been at 0.5 for two days" and "I've only been on oral meds for two days as opposed to the required five" and "Our house may not be ready." Leah simply stated that she had received orders from the powers that be and it was because I was in "excellent" health and stable for my condition. My doctors felt that it was safer for me to be at home in our secluded rural environment as opposed to being exposed to the super-germs of the hospital…and I'm sure a free bed was always appreciated. I guess you should never look a gift horse in the mouth but I really was awfully skeptical about this sudden news. As soon as Leah left I phoned Bob who nearly dropped the receiver as he listened to my news. We arranged that he would arrive by 1:30 p.m. and would bring my Mom who happened to be visiting for a couple of days. He told me later that as soon as he hung up he became a human whirling dervish and cleaned like he had never cleaned before giving my Mom orders as to what her duties were.

While Bob and Mom were at home doing their Mr. & Mrs. Clean thing, I was given instructions as to how to deal with my impending time at home. The first was a sheet detailing the oral medications I was to take and by the look of the quantity, I'd need a suitcase to take them all home! Cyclosporine, which would suppress my immune system so that the new bone marrow would not get into a fight with my body and its organs, was the number one drug I had to take several times daily. Unfortunately, the pill form tasted no different than how the IV form had smelled…dead skunk. You'd think they could have figured out a way to mask its unpalatable properties especially when it had to be swallowed by nauseated patients. In the two days that I had been taking it, I had already learned to hold my breath while quickly gulping water thereby minimizing its unpleasantness. Running in close contention for nastiness was a horse-sized pill called Septra that I was to take three times weekly as well as the ever-present jagged edged fluconazole at four times per day. One folic acid pill at noon was also on the list in addition to a prescription strength antacid called Losec to coat my stomach. Just as a chaser, I was given antinausea pills to take care of any malaise incurred by said pills. I sat staring at the sheet with my eyes glazing over and decided I'd need an administrative assistant to help me remember when and how many to take on a daily basis. What I had no way of knowing was how miserable I was going to feel until the Cyclosporine and Septra were 'tweaked' from a dosage perspective which was to take several weeks. Much emphasis was placed on drinking at least two liters of water per day in order to flush these medications through my kidneys and organs as quickly as possible. When I looked at all these pills and their potential dangers, it was all I could do to swallow them…in a way, I felt as if I was poisoning myself but I knew there was no other viable alternative. The "best" was saved for last. I was handed multiple typed sheets listing possible signs of graft vs. host disease and where and how it might rear its ugly head. There may as well have been skull and crossbones as a header on each page because that is how I viewed it. Basically, it could be anything on your body and the difficult part was identifying whether it was something normal or the first indicator of GVHD. It could show up as an innocent spot or a giant rash or as yellow stool (that I wouldn't have trouble figuring out) or white speckles in the mouth to name a few. I was told I needed to be vigilant and check myself every day and if anything unusual showed up I was to call in immediately and make an appointment to be seen. Talk about putting the fear of God in you! So much for going home…hell, I wanted to stay in the hospital, be safe and have THEM tell me when they saw the first sign of GVHD! I was not only afraid of getting it but also of the drugs that were used to treat it: namely, prednisone. The side effects of prednisone were not pretty….it made you look like a blowfish and that was only what you could see on the outside. What was now deeply rooted into my psyche was an overpowering fear of getting GVHD not to mention the paranoia of waiting for it to show up in one form or another.

For the next few hours, I boxed up my equipment and organized everything that had been my lifeline for four weeks. My room lost its personal touch as I took down all the wonderful cards and pictures that people had sent me leaving only my calendar on the bulletin board...I saw no reason to take that home. In a way, this room had become my Linus's blanket and I had felt safe and protected here. Part of me did not want to leave its security. What did feel strange as I packed up was that I was no longer attached to my pole because I was now on oral medications. My pal, the Hickman was still there though and I wouldn't say goodbye to that until about January 19th which was the 100-day anniversary of its insertion. This was entirely dependent on whether I progressed to the stage where I was no longer in need of any IV transfusions or medications during my outpatient appointments. To start, I had been scheduled for two appointments per week, Tuesdays and Thursdays, and the frequency would depend on how I fared. In a way it was difficult to believe that this journey had only commenced two months prior. I couldn't remember what our lives had been like before that fateful day in Emergency.

At 1:30 p.m. sharp Bob arrived with my Mom. We all hugged in spite of the fact that I was told I shouldn't be doing that…it had after all been five weeks since I had seen my mother. As we were getting my things together, Leah, my lead nurse, came in to say goodbye. She had a special place in my heart and as is normal with a lead nurse, we had become very close during those four weeks sharing many personal conversations and even the odd giggle. I asked Bob to take a picture of Leah and myself.

We said an emotional goodbye and promised to keep in touch, which we did for at least a year. Bob made several trips down to the car and finally the room was empty and it was time to leave the hospital. Dressed in street clothes for the first time in a month, I put on one of Leslie's hats and sat myself down in the wheelchair to be taken downstairs…hospital procedure – but I was too weak to have walked anyway. I honestly do not remember any details of the trip home or what we talked about. I think we were all in shock at the abruptness of my exodus from the hospital.

When we arrived home, Max and Dudley gave me an incredible canine welcome jumping and leaping around.

They say that dogs have no concept of time and whether you are away 20 minutes or 20 days, it makes no difference but I think they were especially excited to see me. Bob kept shushing them away because he was worried that one of them would knock me over…especially Max who weighed about 90 pounds! The last thing we needed was me lying on the floor with Max curiously looking down wondering what I was doing there. After the dogs settled, I gave them a pat ignoring hospital rules both by touching them and allowing them near me. Generally, I adhered to 99% of their restrictions but not having the dogs around was unrealistic…I knew of patients who had to find temporary and sometimes even permanent homes for their pets and we hoped it would not come to that. I figured that if I didn't permit them to lick me or get close to my face, there would be no problems.

Satisfied that the dogs had received their fair share of attention, Bob and Mom carried my belongings into our master bedroom and since this was the most activity I had experienced in four weeks, I had to lie down before I passed out. Bob decided to prepare my dinner while Mom looked after their meal, leaving me alone in bed to contemplate my homecoming. You would think that my first night at home would have been incredibly exciting for all of us but in fact it was the opposite. Perhaps we had thought that once I was back, everything would be magically what it had been when I was healthy but not so; in fact, I felt worse than I had in the hospital. My body was at war with all the new oral medications, and their cumulative effect reminded me of the nausea I had experienced during my week of heavy chemo. I felt like I was back to square one.

Halfway through the meal that Bob had prepared, I said that I could not eat and had to go to bed. I could see the disappointment on their faces but particularly Bob's and as much as it pained me there was nothing I could do but leave the two of them sitting at the table. It broke my heart.

Chapter 15

October 29ᵗʰ to November 30ᵗʰ

The next few days were horribly depressing as the nausea worsened. I could not lie down because I would be sick and at night I had to sit up against pillows to stay on the vertical, which totally ruled out getting any kind of sleep. Out of frustration and fatigue, Bob moved into one of our guest bedrooms because I was constantly trying to get comfortable and this disturbed his attempts at sleep. I couldn't really blame him; he'd had enough of that in the hospital. I had taken the antinausea medication at first but it actually made me feel even worse than just dealing with the nausea alone so I had stopped taking them. It wasn't fair that here I was finally at home and instead of feeling jubilant and healthy, I felt more like a zombie barely able to move and if I did, it was in unbalanced slow motion. My dismal moods and appearance affected Mom and Bob to where even they couldn't smile or laugh and the house became a gloomy environment. One evening, when Mom and I were sitting on the couch waiting for Bob to join us, Mom looked at me and quietly said, "You know Nouchke (her endearment for me) you should try to be more bubbly and happy looking." I looked at her and said, "Mom, it is impossible to be happy when you feel like you are going to throw up every second of the day." My Mom had rarely been ill a day in her life and therefore had no understanding of what it was not to feel well. We left it at that.

Instead of appreciating my time at home, all I wanted to do was get back to the hospital for my first appointment on Tuesday where I hoped that my doctors would sort out why I was so nauseated. One of the items that had been listed on the sheaf of sheets as a potential sign of GHVD was, in fact, nausea stemming from rejection in the stomach. That possibility was weighing heavily on my mind. Even though I felt terribly sick, I'd get out of bed every hour to look at myself in the mirror, examining each speck and spot on my body or in my mouth. One of Bob's responsibilities was to do a full body check once a day and inspect me for any unusual markings or discolorations. I'd stand there with bated breath in terrified anticipation of whether he discovered something. Each day seemed like 48 hours; I couldn't eat, I couldn't sleep, I couldn't get out of bed except to check for GVHD and I actually began to think back fondly to my isolation room where I had been safe. How crazy was that?

Tuesday could not arrive quickly enough. In the morning, Bob and I set out for our appointment in 3Z and we dropped off Mom en route at the commuter train station so that she could go home. Because it was not unusual for a transplant patient to receive blood or platelet transfusions even after the transplant, we had been warned that depending on what I needed, it was possible to spend the entire day at the hospital. When we arrived in 3Z, the nurses took my blood and Bob volunteered to take it down to the lab along with several other patients' vials. Before too long, the nurses received my hemoglobin and platelets results and they were thrilled with the numbers. Pat's marrow was doing its job and they had increased steadily since my last test at the hospital the day of my discharge. My white cells had taken a tumble but that was to be expected because the growth stimulator gave only a momentary boost and from now on, these cells had to increase on their own as the marrow became more ensconced. The tests did show that I needed a bag of magnesium which was quite normal and that product was promptly ordered. I had also been tested for CMV (*Cytomegalovirus*) as part of the routine bone marrow transplant procedure. This is a member of the herpes virus family and 50-85% of the population in the United States has had some type of CMV infection by age 40. Mostly the infection goes unnoticed in healthy people, and may be as simple as a cold sore. In others, it can exhibit "mono" type symptoms which eventually go away. In infants or bone marrow transplant patients, however, it can be a deadly virus and the treatment for it is almost as lethal. Part of the protocol was to test for this during my outpatient appointments. It was possible to contract CMV from someone but, typically, it appeared after transplant because the donor had been CMV positive. Sadly, if you only had a choice of one donor and they had the CMV virus, then that was it or that was it! Miraculously, Pat and I had tested negative...another astounding detail about our match. At least I would not have to worry about that in addition to GVHD. All the patients waited with great trepidation for their blood results. It was like a lottery gone awry in some bizarre Twilight Zone episode as you waited to find out if you were the unlucky winner. Would you have CMV, GVHD (certain cells could indicate its presence) or worse yet, if you were a leukemia patient, had your cancer returned? One cannot comprehend what a horror this was for all concerned unless you have sat in one of those vinyl chairs in that outpatient room. Everyone breathed a giant sigh of relief when their results indicated none of these things, only to have to go through it all again during their next appointment. I honestly wonder how we survived...I guess there is no alternative and you just cope with what comes your way.

While I was receiving my magnesium transfusion, Nancy and her husband walked in. We had only ever seen each other through my window and had never spoken, but now even though we had our masks on we recognized each other. She sat next to me and we chatted about how we were feeling and how our first few days at home had been since our mutual discharges.

Nancy commented that I seemed more energetic than her and truth be told, I had noticed when she had entered the room, that she appeared more tired than me. Our big topic of discussion was GVHD and whether either of us had discovered any signs of it. Only another transplant patient in the same circumstance could understand the daily fear of wondering whether today was THE day when you would find it on some part of your body. Once the rejection began, who knew where it would lead and if it could be stopped?

As we talked, I watched the nurses move from one patient to the next. Usually, they each had a cart that held bandages, scissors, rubber gloves, antibiotic, disinfectant and the like and they moved it from patient to patient. One of the nurse's duties during these appointments was to clean the incisions and flush the tubing of each patient's Hickman. While I had been in isolation, this had been done daily and always caused much pain because the skin around the incisions had never healed properly and had actually begun to tear away each time a bandage was pulled off. I looked forward to this about as much as "getting my finger caught in a car door"...one of Bob's favorite expressions. There was no way around the discomfort, though, because the risk for infection from the Hickman was high and consequently there was no escaping its cleaning and flushing. There we sat, women and men alike. The nurses did an excellent job of being discreet while working on the women whose Hickmans were in their chest so that no breast area was exposed for anyone else to see. By mid-afternoon my transfusion was finished and we were ready to go home. We had a two-day reprieve until my return on Thursday. Once I had been home for a few weeks and no longer came for weekly visits, Bob was taught to clean the incision areas of the Hickman. It was a 30-minute endeavor for a non-professional. Bob was very intense when he performed this ritual and I would squirm around because my skin was still extremely raw. I dreaded having it done and he similarly did not look forward to doing it because of my histrionics, no doubt, as he always felt that he was hurting me. The hospital had arranged for a home care nurse to do the flushing because it was more complicated. I had to give Bob credit for taking the bull by the horns and accepting the responsibility; I doubted that there were many spouses who volunteered for that job.

For the following 14 days, we lived from appointment to appointment. During my next visit, my blood tests indicated that my kidney chemistry was out of whack and I was chastised for not drinking enough water so that all the medications would be flushed through my system. I thought to myself that I would drown if I drank another ounce of H_2O! Upon further investigation, it was discovered that a dosage error had been made in the antibiotic called Septra and that this was the culprit for my nausea and kidney trouble. Once that was regulated, my nausea virtually disappeared and I was able to eat again which helped me gain a bit of stamina. It's not that I could do a lot, but I was able to start doing some small household chores like laundry, emptying the dishwasher and such. What was frustrating was for every five minutes I worked, I would have to lie down for half an hour. If I pushed myself and worked too hard ignoring my fatigue, I would be in bed for an entire day as a consequence. Never in my life had I not been able to work nonstop and I had to learn to live in a different, less compulsive way, which for me was perhaps not a bad thing.

Even though sleep was elusive, my energy level low and the fear of GVHD still present, there were moments of laughter and times when our lives felt slightly normal. Because of my time in the hospital and the fact that I was physically unable, Bob had taken over the grocery shopping responsibility which was quite funny since he hadn't done that in over 25 years. I'd give him a grocery list and frequently he would call from the grocery store asking what type of parmesan cheese to buy or which brand of deli bread was the better one. I'd laugh when he got home as he complained about the line ups at the register or how slow his cashier had been…it was like I was listening to myself. Slowly I began to cook and enjoy eating once again. My mouth sores were still there but had not increased and if I was careful, I could eat as long as the food wasn't too hot in temperature or spicy in flavor. That was a bit of a problem for me since I loved a steaming, fiery spiced meal and had to constantly refrain out of habit from adding too much hot sauce or pepper flakes. In my previous life, I could use a third of a bottle of Tabasco Sauce in a Bloody Mary! Those days were long gone. Bob was ecstatic that I had taken over the cooking once again and he appreciated my dinners even more, savoring each mouthful and inhaling the aroma as he never had before. While I was making supper, he would come into the kitchen and give me a long hug saying nothing…there were no words that could express how grateful he was that I was alive.

During my second week at home, our friend Owen invited Bob for lunch. We had been friends for fifteen years and even though he was younger than Bob and I, our mutual love of excellent cuisine, fine wine (not to mention loving a good laugh) made ours a unique relationship. When Owen arrived, he stayed in our front hallway and we said hello from a distance not wanting to risk any germ or bacteria transfer. From his darting eyes, I could tell that he was having trouble reconciling this bald, bathrobe clad, gaunt, pale woman to the Esther he had always known. In usual Owen style, he cracked a few jokes and instantly lifted my spirits…it felt good to laugh. When they were ready to leave, Bob kissed me goodbye more of an air kiss really (out of necessity) and reminded me that he could be reached by cell phone should there by ANY problems. As they walked out the door, so did my momentary elation and the gloom of being cut off once again enveloped me and I began to cry. Even our house had turned into a prison: yes, it was a vast improvement over my room in isolation, but it was still solitary confinement and I was unable to come and go as I pleased. I knew Bob needed a break but I was actually jealous of his ability to be with friends and go to a restaurant...I could barely remember what that had been like. Suddenly the doorbell rang and jolted me out of my misery. A florist's delivery man stood at the door and before I could tell him that I could not accept any flowers, he stated that he had an arrangement from Owen with very special instructions. I was perplexed by this as I watched him walk back to his van. He returned carrying a monstrous black urn filled with a breathtaking evergreen display completely decorated with battery operated Christmas lights!!! He set the urn outside our front door and gave me a knowing smile...no doubt Owen had given him a heads up. This sweet man explained that Owen had supplied the urn and lights and they had done the rest. Now, instead of tears of desperation, tears of joy filled my eyes as I thanked him and said goodbye. Owen's thoughtfulness and inventiveness as well as the timing of the delivery will never be forgotten as long as I live. I immediately called Bob and asked to speak to Owen so I could thank him from the bottom of my heart. Owen was delighted that I was as thrilled as he had anticipated and explained that his idea had been to come up with an outside floral arrangement that could be seen through our front door or window. Indeed that was the case as it shone magnificently at night putting a smile on my face each time I looked at it.

That was a highlight in those first four weeks. Each day was fraught with worry about getting GVHD and the stress increased as more and more patients that I knew came down with various forms of it. During one of my hospital visits, I saw a woman who looked like a burn victim completely covered with angry, oozing wounds indicating that the new bone marrow had waged war on her skin, the largest organ of one's body. It had all started with a seemingly innocent rash and had escalated to this terrifying sight. Seeing this only fueled my paranoia and I began to examine myself two to three times per hour, sometimes even with a magnifying glass if I wasn't sure what I was seeing. You have no idea how many normal changes occur on oneself in the course of a day or week until you start keeping track of them. Every pimple, mole, skin discoloration, freckle that I saw, I examined multiple times wondering if this was IT. One day I even took a picture of some strange looking discolored skin on my knee so that I could compare the picture with my knee on a daily basis and see if it enlarged. Bob had to humor me each day when I asked him to look at something more closely and tell me what he thought it was and on more than one occasion he would storm out of the room in frustration. I knew I was carrying it all too far but I could not control myself. I think I can understand why some marriages disintegrate under this kind of endless pressure. I realize now that I should have sought professional counseling…no one could have gone through what I went through without bearing lifelong psychological scars.

By the end of November, my twice a week checkups had been reduced to once every second week which was practically unheard of for a patient with only four weeks under their belt since engraftment. I was doing exceptionally well from a CBC (complete blood count) perspective and other than my consistently low white cell count, everything else was in the normal range and my doctors were thrilled. I was told repeatedly how unusual it was that I had no complications and how lucky I was to have excellent blood counts, but my preoccupation with GVHD dampened my zeal. Overall though, I was feeling more energetic and during one of my visits, I decided to ask Kathy, my acute care nurse practitioner, if I would be able to leave the house soon and perhaps go grocery shopping. The time had come. She advised me that I could go as long as I wore a mask, went in non-peak times and washed my hands immediately upon returning home. Kathy didn't really need to emphasize the hand washing part because Bob and I virtually had no skin left from washing them so frequently. Bob told me daily that he couldn't bear the thought of washing his sore hands one more time.

Over the course of that first month there were many disappointments with regard to my slow recovery...at least that was the way I viewed it. I remember carefully going down the stairs to our basement and returning with a pantry item and by the time I got back upstairs, I had to lie down. It was very discouraging and I wondered how I would ever get back into shape. You would think that I would have been satisfied with my excellent progress and the fact that I had survived to this point, but I guess the human spirit always wants more...at least mine anyway. One day I decided, with Bob's support, that it was time for me to take a walk around our acreage...my first venture outside. It was a brisk, clear day with a light dusting of snow on the ground. I dressed myself like the abominable snow-woman; ski jacket, boots, hat, gloves and even a mask! I tended to take instruction to the extreme as was my nature. I had been told to be careful not only about what I breathed in, but also about my exposure to the sun. UVA and UVB rays could damage my skin bringing on a GVHD reaction and having seen the lady with the oozing wounds, I was not about to put myself in that kind of jeopardy. If I did get GVHD, it wouldn't be because I had made a stupid mistake. To this day, six years later, I always wear SPF 70 to protect my skin.

When I walked outside, I was both afraid and happy. Slowly I plodded across our back pasture to the fence perimeter while Max and Dudley ran back and forth as if to keep an eye on me. Even the little amount of snow made the walk more of an effort and I had to stop every few steps to catch my breath from the exertion. In the distance, I could see Bob watching me...little did I know he was crying as he observed my slow, labored progress. With each painful step that I took, I could feel my feet crackling and I remembered that Janet had said to be careful because after two months of immobility there was a chance of breaking those very fragile bones. I had always been a power walker and now it was agony just to put one foot in front of the other. As Bob watched my slow progress, I'm sure he could not grasp that this was me; I had always walked so fast that he often told me during our walks together, that if I didn't slow down, he would never go with me again. When I reached the house, I was ready to keel over!

In the fourth week of November, even though my white cell count was still well below normal, I announced to Bob that I was going grocery shopping. Bob was worried but he knew that for my sanity as well as his, I had to venture out into the world and begin living again. I felt totally elated at this simple task of what most people considered drudgery. Just before entering the supermarket, I put on a mask and boldly walked through the automatic doors to pick up a cart which I carefully disinfected with Sani-Wipes. I had never thought about a shopping cart as being a festering vehicle of bacteria but that was certainly how I viewed it now...especially the area where the infants and toddlers sat with their leaky diapers. Why had I ever put groceries THERE...the thought had never occurred to me until my medical team had given me the Do's and Don'ts about my daily life! Most shoppers would not even look at me, in fact they took a wide berth if I was near them. It always amazed me that they thought I was the one with something contagious as opposed to the other way around. Many times I thought about having a T-shirt made with some kind of glib comment like, "The mask is for your germs – not mine!"

The good news about having a near death experience is that I began to see everything in a new light. What did hit me about these shopping expeditions was that most people were either unhappy-looking or always in a hurry. I felt like telling them, "You should be appreciative to be shopping and be out and about when others can't even get out of their hospital beds or house!" They probably would have hit me with an acorn squash if I had been brazen enough to make such a comment. It was all I could do at times not to say something. In a way I was like a reformed smoker, only now it was about noticing how many people took absolutely everything around them for granted and didn't realize how precious even the small, mundane things were.

Chapter 16

December 1ˢᵗ to January 31ˢᵗ

December arrived and with it, holiday celebrations. Cautiously a semblance of a social life returned. The rule was that if someone came over, they immediately had to wash their hands upon entry and they would not be allowed to come over if they felt the least bit unwell. Needless to say, the no-kissing rule applied too, which still does to this day unless it is on the cheek. In the first week of December, our annual Christmas dinner with Mike and his wife, Chris, was arranged. We thought long and hard about whether I should go out and we discussed it with "my people" at the hospital. Their advice was: go only to a restaurant you trust in terms of hygiene whether it was food preparation or surroundings, and do not go to any family restaurants because of the child/germ factor. In addition, buffets were totally taboo for a person with a low immune system! My doctors viewed those serving trays and the warmed food they contained for hours and hours as giant incubating vessels for all sorts of food microorganisms. Keeping all of those restrictions in mind, I chose an upscale restaurant that we had frequented and phoned to make a reservation. Because we were regular patrons, I felt comfortable explaining my condition and requested a table not too near another. The manager was very accommodating and said he would do his best.

On December 6ᵗʰ, the evening was made even more special when we were chauffeured to the restaurant in a stretch limousine. I was nicely dressed and had opted to go without a hat other than wearing one for warmth while stepping from the limo to the restaurant. Once inside, we left our outerwear at the coat check and all eyes followed us as we were led to a table that had been placed at least 15 feet away from anyone else with a beautiful view of the water and the twinkling Christmas lights outside. I'm sure our observers wondered why we deserved such special treatment and no doubt speculated as to whether I was bald due to illness or simply making a fashion statement. The fact that my baldness suited me kept most people

guessing. It was a memorable evening and for the first time in what seemed an eternity I forgot about my illness and viewed myself as a human being and not a patient.

During these weeks, I continued to have my daily evening conversations with Mom, Pat and Linda. Since everyone was healthy and I was improving daily, we decided to have them all over to our house for dinner and an overnight the second week of December. I had not seen Pat and Linda for almost two months since transplant day and we were all looking forward to seeing each other. The unique bond between Pat and I had only intensified...we were truly joined at the hip now. The day of their arrival was a memorable occasion. Pat took pictures of me every few minutes seizing the moment thinking perhaps, that nothing should be put off until tomorrow because one never knew what might happen. They joked about my appearance and that with the stubble on my head I resembled a popular female rock star. Shortly after we settled in, Bob presented Pat with a truly special gift that Bob had chosen especially for him. Pat was speechless, as were Linda and Mom, and he looked at us saying he could not accept it. This did not surprise me because I knew he felt we were somehow demeaning what he had done for me by giving him something in return. After much pleading, and explaining that this was only a small way for us to express our gratitude did he reluctantly accept the gift. Bob had no other way of demonstrating how very thankful he was that I was alive and I hoped that Pat understood.

My general mass emailings continued to friends and family who had been on my mailing list during my time in the hospital, although the frequency now had lessened to once every couple of weeks or when there was something particularly significant to convey. Let's face it…people have to get on with their own lives and I felt that enough was enough. Excepted were close friends and family whom I still communicated with several times per week. One morning, an email from Leslie was in my inbox saying that she thought I would get a kick out of the picture she had enclosed. I opened the attachment and staring at me was a lovely, youthful girl in her late teens with short streaked hair. Leslie and I had worked together as young women and it was an old picture of me when I was nineteen. Sitting there looking at myself…vibrant, healthy, and oh so naïve, never fathoming what the future would hold, I began to weep. I wept for the injustices in life, the hardships that Bob and I had endured and for the loss of my innocence. My innocence from the perspective of having no awareness that life could change in a blink…one minute the world was your oyster and the next you were deathly ill and faced with oblivion and if you survived, your life would never be the same. Now I lived my life in constant fear that I would be hospitalized again or worse yet, die from some complication due to GVHD. Bob walked in while I was sobbing and he held me while I tried to explain about the picture. Poor Leslie had sent it with good intent and couldn't have imagined that this would be my reaction.

Leading up to Christmas, brought more socializing but for as many times as something was arranged, we had to cancel because our friends would call and say that they had a cold or flu. Sometimes it wasn't even that they themselves were sick but that a family member was ill and they were concerned that they might be contagious even though they were not showing any symptoms. We appreciated their conscientiousness and made the best of it when we did have people over. Usually, when friends visited they wanted to contribute by bringing a food item so that I would not be overloaded with work. That offer was not made lightly because they had to follow strict food preparation guidelines so that whatever they cooked would not contaminate me in any way shape or form. Refrigeration of food, cleanliness of surfaces and the careful washing of fruits and vegetables to name a few, were just some of things that had to be considered. Jim's wife, Debbie, said that she nearly went into apoplexy worrying about what she prepared so that it would be totally safe for me to eat.

Mom celebrated Christmas with us and it was a peaceful few days. We had not exchanged gifts for many years, but an exception was made considering the special circumstances. Bob surprised me with a beautiful DSLR Nikon camera. One of my passions had always been photography and I was delighted with this gift but more so by what it represented. Mom, also breaking tradition, gave me a black knit top that she had bought in the early stages of my illness…buying it gave her hope that I would be "around" at Christmas. With Mom's help, Bob enjoyed a full turkey dinner which included mashed potatoes, squash and apples, green beans, homemade stuffing and gravy of course! I had a decent appetite by then and ate everything minus the turkey. Pat would joke and ask if I'd had any cravings for steak yet. I guess deep down he hoped that given his bone marrow I would give up being a vegetarian. (I have, six years later.) He mentioned that he pictured me standing at the BBQ cooking a plate-sized steak, beer in hand and scratching my "You know whats!" I laughed heartily at that comment. We did have an interesting coincidence though...many a night I would find myself having uncontrollable cravings for potato chips at bedtime. Chips had always been my weakness but I had never eaten anything in bed and if I did, it would certainly not be greasy, crumbly chips. I mentioned to Linda about the evening snack and that I had been going to bed with potato chips and she said...Pat does that every night!!! It made me pause and wonder...

By January, my appointments were reduced to once a month and this was monumental for a transplant patient of my tenure. Most of the people that I had met were still going for weekly if not twice per week appointments. I was beginning to feel some "survivor's guilt" at how well I was doing and mentioned this to Kathy and Tina during one of my appointments. They looked at me in disbelief and said that if it weren't for people such as me who did well and survived, what would the reward be for their hard work and dedication? I took that to heart but I did downplay to other patients how I felt when asked. How could you boast about it when many of them literally looked like death warmed over and were dealing with the ravages of Acute GVHD?

It was in this period of my recovery that I became even more fearful of GVHD if that was even possible. Now that I had a semblance of health again, I became selfish about it and did not want to lose it! The obsession with GVHD increased so much so, that Bob and I were having arguments over it and I eventually stopped asking his opinion if I saw something suspicious. It wasn't that it was bothersome for him to look but it was just that every time I asked him, he too would worry about whether I had a rejection problem. I knew I had to get this under control and decided to speak with Kathy, my acute care nurse practitioner during my next appointment. I rarely saw Dr. Wasi anymore which was positive because her precious time was reserved for the patients in dire need...she would occasionally come in during my time with Kathy and say hello and comment on how well I was doing. When I saw Kathy, I told her about my GVHD phobia and she recommended a psychologist that was familiar with the challenges that bone marrow transplant patients had. If I had been her, I would have been thinking... why are you agonizing over GVHD that you don't even have when other people who do have it, are coping with it!!!!!!!!??? Kathy gave me a doctor's name and phone number. Bob was pleased that I had chosen to seek professional help but in the end, I never called her...sort of like the open door in my isolation room...once I had the option, I decided to deal with it myself and as time went on, the anxiety decreased. I realize now that I should have found a counselor to help me deal with these fears...yes, the anxiety decreased but when faced with various normal health issues as part of middle age, my terror of being sick returns. I realize now that my mind needed healing as well as my body, and now six years later I have sought counselling.

During these weeks of appointments, I did see Nancy the odd time and we also communicated via email. She was still going for weekly appointments and sometime in January, I received an email from her saying that she was to be re-admitted because she had been diagnosed with CMV (*Cytomegalovirus*). This was every bone marrow transplant patient's worst nightmare, to have to go back into the hospital and especially with something like CMV. The treatment, as I mentioned before, was dreadfully dangerous and given a transplant patient's delicate state, the outcome could be deadly. While Nancy was back in the hospital, I dropped in for a visit during one of my routine appointments. The differences in our recovery were even more notable now. She could barely walk and her speech was slurred, probably due to the drugs she was on to combat the CMV. I wondered whether she would survive. Nancy told me that she was urinating blood and constantly nauseated. How could a human being withstand the constant barrage of toxic medications? Why, after everything she had been through, did she deserve this? I often thought how unfair life was and why certain people had to suffer like this.

Nancy was not the only one who was in trouble; she was one of several. A young French Canadian woman who also had leukemia and had a transplant the previous month, was told her leukemia had returned. She underwent another bout of chemotherapy in an effort to battle the cancer but in the end, she gave up and left to die peacefully at home. She was only 29. These were the kinds of stories I heard each time I went to 3Z for my appointments. It's not that I had to worry about leukemia but each patient's battle affected me as if it were my own. Would I ever just be able to live without wondering if and when I would be dealt another bad hand of cards?

On January 19th my Hickman was removed. I had dreaded the procedure but as a pleasant surprise, it turned out to be a piece of cake! As the surgeon finished taking out the Hickman, he apologized at the fact that there might be slight scarring where he was stitching up the entry and exit incisions. I thought to myself, "Hey Doc, what are a few scars…I AM ALIVE and that is the last thing I am worried about." From now on, any blood taking would have to be done the old-fashioned way…with a regular needle. I didn't mind that inconvenience one little bit because I would no longer need the Hickman cleaned or flushed or have to worry about getting it caught in my clothes and ripped out by accident. No Hickman also meant that I would be able to start horseback riding again. My doctors were not too pleased about this but I promised them that I would not enter our barn (mold issues) and that I would ride in our indoor arena away from the hay and horse feces. They knew that by the set of my jaw, my decision had been made. In the third week of January, only three months after my transplant, I rode one of our calmer horses for ten minutes. I have to be honest and say that I was extremely nervous riding again. What would the repercussions be if I fell off and was seriously injured? I tried not to think about it as I rode and only concentrated on the job at hand. Normally, I would have been able to ride and train for at least an hour without stopping, but by the end of those few short minutes, I was spent. Bob was thrilled that I had ridden…it was a monumental baby step in the right direction.

Chapter 17

February 1ˢᵗ to April 30ᵗʰ

Many days throughout these first few months of my recovery brought frustrating challenges due to the restrictions I had to follow. The incessant need for cleanliness whether it was food preparation or personal hygiene made everything time-consuming and complicated. A simple trip to the grocery store, now without a mask, became a logistical nightmare. During the shopping trip itself, if I heard someone coughing in another aisle or saw children, I would detour and go to another section, similarly if people stood in line at the checkout and they sounded sick, I'd leave and return later. When I returned home and unloaded the groceries; everything that I had touched had to be disinfected – from door handles, to the knobs on the cupboards to the refrigerator handle. Bob and I cringed at the prospect of washing and rewashing our hands as our skin became more and more tender. Even a short time outside meant having to cover up with either clothing or sunscreen regardless of the fact that it was only winter…the sun's rays had to be avoided at all times.

As much as I tried to control it, my life revolved around fear, my new four letter "F" word…fear of infection, fear of GVHD, fear of those around me. The flip side of the "fear coin" was complete appreciation of being alive regardless of the angst. I began to view everything in a new light… much like a toddler's delight at being able to walk for the first time and having a whole new world within reach. Previously, I had been so busy running down the road with blinders on that I had never taken the time to truly appreciate the ones I loved or to smell the roses. Whether it was saying "I Love You" on the phone, listening to the song of a robin or watching an incredible sunset, I now spent more time on what is important. Given a choice between balancing my bank statement or having that extra cup of coffee with Bob, I choose the latter...in my former life I would have been compelled to do the work first.

As the weeks passed, my visits to the hospital remained monthly because my white cells were still below normal. The good news was that all my other counts were excellent and almost every number in my blood chemistry was perfect. I could not have asked for anything more. As part of routine procedure with a bone marrow transplant patient that had an opposite sex donor, a test was done to determine what percentage of my chromosomes had become male...yes, you read that correctly. The result would indicate how thorough the engraftment was. When Kathy read me the results, it was like finding out you were adopted and who you thought you were, you were really not at all...my chromosomes were 99.9% male. This was a good thing apparently because it meant that Pat's marrow had fully engrafted into mine. Not only had my chromosomes changed but my blood type had gone from B Negative to Pat's which was B Positive...and that is what I aim for to "be positive." Other than having the ability to commit the perfect murder with no one being able to identify me, there were no physical repercussions from my DNA changes. A Bone Marrow Transplant is symbolized by a butterfly and represents the transformation, or metamorphosis, that a patient undergoes once engraftment is successful. There was no doubt that I had been transformed.

In March, Mom celebrated her 74th birthday and we invited her to spend a few days with us at the farm. It was typical March weather, or "Farch" as we call it...the ground was covered by several inches of slushy snow but the days had lost that ice-cold feel of January and February. One afternoon, I decided Mom and I should take a walk down the road where there was a spectacular mini-waterfall that she had never seen before. This was part of my new philosophy of spending more time on the important things…like an afternoon with your mother. Since we were walking in the sloppy snow, I had to find some clothes and footwear for Mom because she did not own a single piece of "farm" clothing as she called it. Her closet only contained dresses, skirts, blouses and HIGH-HEELED SHOES. We were constantly chastising her for not wearing sensible footwear to which she'd comment …"If I ever get to the stage where I can't wear high-heeled shoes, I'll be dead." I dug through my closet and supplied Mom with a ripped, old ski jacket, a pair of pants and tall green rubber boots and I was dressed more or less the same which was quite normal for me on the farm. Bob photographed us as we stood outside, arm in arm, splaying out our toes as if we were a couple of clowns. We laughed till we thought we would fall over at the sight of my mother in particular wearing such an outfit. In the evening, we went out for dinner to a quaint, local restaurant that we hadn't been to since before my illness in August. When we were seated at our table, a young waiter who had served us months before greeted us saying that it had been a while and he liked my new, short hair style. (My hair was about an inch long.) Mom, Bob and I looked at each other and for a moment we were at a loss for words at the complete innocence of the statement. It made my day because this meant I did not look as sick as I thought…just someone with a new hair style.

Even with my steady improvements and all the positive reinforcements from my doctors and nurses that I was "on my way," I remained nerve-racked as a result of the routine hospital visits. In April, during one of my appointments, I saw Nancy in the outpatient room. I walked over to where she was sitting and knelt in front of her because there were no chairs available. All we could see were each other's eyes because we were still required to wear face masks. I asked her how she was doing and she said, "It's back." For a brief moment, I did not compute what she was talking about but then I realized what the "It" was. Her leukemia had resurfaced. We both had tears in our eyes and I held her hands in mine. I asked her what the next step was and she said she had been given the option of participating in some experimental trials and she would give that serious consideration. When you were offered "experimental trials" you knew your options were getting close to nil. My heart ached for her. Since her transplant, she had not had one "well" moment what with the CMV episode and now this. I hugged her when I left and asked her to please email and keep me posted as to her decision. Talk about "survivor's guilt"…how I felt at that moment was beyond words. Little did I know that would be the last time we would see each other. I kept asking myself why was I so lucky and not she? If there was a master plan to people's lives, I could not grasp the logic of why this should happen to anyone. Had she not been through enough? I was outraged at the unfairness of it all, the pain and misery inflicted on an innocent person. Nancy had struggled through eight months of chemo prior to her transplant to oust the leukemia and then the process of the transplant itself which was a "killer" followed by CMV treatment. I simply did not get IT! Bob was terribly upset as well and we left the hospital totally depressed. A couple of weeks later I received an email from Nancy saying she had decided not to participate in the trial and she was going home. She would deal with her local hospital for any palliative care…she was giving up. I could not argue with her decision and would have done the same in her shoes. I had experienced those exact feelings prior to my transplant… there comes a time when as much as you love those around you, it's no longer about them it's about what is right for you. She had reached that point. Our communications dwindled to nothing after that. How could we keep writing each other? There was nothing left to say.

By the end of April, I was horseback riding three to four days per week at one-hour stretches and I had taken over most of my

housework again, as well as the bookkeeping function in our business. I was fortunate that I was able to do most of my work from home which reduced my exposure to any germs and bacteria. On the odd occasion when I did go in, Vicki would completely sanitize my office, taking her responsibility seriously of preserving my health status. I enjoyed having a routine again but had not lost sight of my newfound self and created a good balance between work and pleasure, with pleasure being the winner more often than not. At one point, Bob proposed a trip to celebrate my upcoming birthday on April 26th and suggested we return to Vancouver Island for a few days as had been our tradition in past years. I was skeptical at first but knew that since this would be a domestic trip, it was a good way to wet my feet in terms of travel and still be safe. We arranged to stay in several B&B's and flew out on April 23rd. Truthfully, I was terrified of being out in the "real" world with all of its unseen dangers. While we were away, we washed our hands about 50 times a day and if I was near someone that either coughed or sneezed I held my breath until I was out of range of being contaminated. It's a wonder I didn't turn blue or faint.

In retrospect, being away was more stressful than being at home but these leaps had to be taken in order to resume semblances of our former life. What did make the trip memorable was the morning of my birthday.

We were in a quaint B&B and our room had a breathtaking view overlooking the Pacific Ocean. To make the event even more special, Bob had arranged with the staff for a bottle of champagne to be served with our in-room breakfast of eggs benedict and fresh fruit. As Bob was taking some photos of me, champagne glass in hand, there was a knock at the door. When Bob answered, a humongous crystal vase filled with beautiful flowers obliterated the individual who had brought it. Behind this person, was another carrying a bottle of incredibly expensive French champagne. They handed Bob an envelope no doubt wondering who the sender was of such an opulent gift. Bob and I opened the card, which read, "I am happy that you are here to be there! Love, Owen." As always, Owen had touched my heart with his thoughtfulness and sensitivity. Afterwards, he told us that he knew I would insist on taking the flowers from hotel to hotel and he laughed at the thought of us carrying a large, glass vase from one place to the next. It was hilarious to see the expression on the people's faces at the reception desk when we checked into our subsequent inns. By the time we got to the last one, we had left the vase behind and it had been replaced by an empty salsa jar which held one remaining orchid stem. I had made it through our first venture away from home unscathed but I was very happy to get back to my safety net.

All in all, life was returning to normal gradually even with the anxiety of worrying about GVHD. When I went to the hospital and was faced with other patients and their problems, it would resurface in full force. Once I was home for a couple of weeks, it would ebb. One visit in particular set me back immensely and it took me weeks to get a hold of myself again. I had met a leukemia patient about my age and during one of my appointments, we began to talk and compare recoveries as was inevitable. I still had no complications at this point other than a low white cell count and I was asked by this lady if I had any rejection problems. I answered that I had not and she divulged that her skin had been affected by GVHD and offered her forearm for me to touch. I nearly recoiled at the feel of it because instead of skin, I felt something similar to hard, smooth plastic. She told me that other parts of her body including her stomach area were becoming as stiff as her arm and she was on immune suppressing drugs to help curb the spread. I was shocked and after we said goodbye, I spent the entire time in the waiting room pinching my arms and legs wondering if I had the beginnings of this type of GVHD…of course I did not. As soon as I got home, I went on the internet, worst thing you can do by the way, and found out that what she had was called Scleroderma an auto immune disorder that can occur in bone marrow transplant patients as a result of GVHD. For weeks, I checked myself in the mirror, top to bottom, side to side feeling my skin dozens of times a day…I nearly had a nervous breakdown.

Chapter 18

May 1ˢᵗ to June 30ᵗʰ

In May, Bob and I began discussing a promise that he had made when I had been hospitalized and in isolation. He had said that he would throw a party for all of our family and key friends who had been such tremendous support during my battle as a celebration of my survival. Now, six months later, it seemed that he would be able to fulfill his promise. Knowing that I would want to organize it myself, he handed me the reins and gave me carte blanche as to the arrangements. We decided it would be held at our favorite restaurant in the first week of June and I met with the chef/owner to make the menu choices. Twenty invitations were sent out and I coined the party "Celebration of Life." Bob and I looked forward to the event and being able to share our joy with everyone.

Later that month, Owen came over for dinner and we began discussing the fact that he had taken several cycling vacations and was planning to book another one in Burgundy, France in the fall. Bob had never been keen on this idea because our way to see the world was usually on horseback, but because of my lack of strength and the danger involved in an equine vacation, he was open to giving a cycling trip a try. It was decided that the three of us would go to Burgundy in September and Bob and I made a pact to spend the summer training in order to get in shape for a week's worth of cycling.

Life was getting back on track. My monthly appointments had not changed in frequency but there was a reduction in most of the medication that I was on except for Cyclosporine, the anti-rejection drug. Dr. Wasi wanted me to be on this drug until she felt that there was absolutely no chance of rejection. With leukemia patients, they did want a small amount of GVHD present because GVHD actually destroyed some leukemia cells and this phenomenon is referred to as "Graft vs. Leukemia" effect. In my case however, since my blood disorder was not a cancer, the doctors did not want me getting any GVHD reaction. The dangers were too great. Of interest, is the fact that a bone marrow transplant is the only organ transplant that if successful, the patient will not need to be on life-long anti-rejection drugs…for any other type of transplant, the person is on drugs forevermore. As afraid as I was of getting any GVHD, I was beginning to get anxious about getting off the cyclosporine. I knew there were many side effects from the drug and especially from long-term use. From a strictly cosmetic standpoint, in me it had promoted increased hair growth on my face and arms and believe me, I didn't need that. I actually had tufts of hair along the sides of my cheeks close to my ear lobes which made me feel like a stray tomcat! It's not that I cared what I looked like because I had lived and that was all that mattered but a bit less hair would have been nice! The flip side of the coin was that the hair on my head was growing in well and I had already gone for several haircuts to help shape it as it was getting longer. Interestingly, my hair was completely gray and soft as a baby's bottom as it grew. Over time the color returned to what it had been before my chemo with only the normal amount of gray for my age…I have chosen not to color it anymore because I do not choose to expose myself to any more chemicals than absolutely necessary.

June came and we eagerly awaited my Celebration of Life party. Mom, Pat, Linda, Leslie, and Jim and Debbie would stay at our house. Everyone had cameras and hundreds of pictures were taken. Pat and I felt like a couple of movie stars as cameras clicked away.

All the other guests had booked hotels nearby and would arrive for cocktails at the restaurant at 6:00 p.m. I had taken advantage of Bob's "carte blanche" philosophy and had ordered a stretch limo to take the group staying at our house, as well as Owen, to the restaurant. On the way there, we joked and laughed and drank champagne…it felt good to forget everything if only for an evening. Nearly everyone that was invited attended, some came from far away, others not, and as I sat at our table looking around the restaurant I considered myself a very fortunate person to have so many wonderful people that cared about me and Bob. Both Bob and I gave a short speech just before dinner expressing our heartfelt thanks with specific mention made to Pat of course. During my speech, I made a tribute to my "knight in shining armor" who had stood by me through thick and thin. The evening was a giant success.

Left to Right: Mom, Andrew, Janet, Pat, Linda and Bob.

A week after my party, the transplant ward held its annual picnic for the patients. Because the ward was such a close knit group and the whole procedure of the bone marrow transplant very unique, a picnic seemed an excellent venue to get together in something other than a hospital environment. This particular one was special because it marked the 25 year celebration of the inception of the transplant program at McMaster University Hospital. There were more transplant patients than normal in attendance at the picnic because of its significant anniversary. Friends and family were encouraged to come and especially the donors for the transplants. For the most part, if donors attended, they were usually the related ones because non-related donors could come from anywhere in the world and it was not realistic for them to attend. Also, the identity of non-related donors was not revealed until one year after transplant and in some cases, the donor preferred to stay anonymous. The related donors always outnumbered the non-related ones at the picnics. Pat and Linda were part of this auspicious group and I was extremely proud to introduce them to fellow patients and hospital staff. In honor of the anniversary, all the patients were given silver balloons and were asked to stand in a group on a large, grassy area.

Esther, in the back row, three to the left of lady in the wheelchair.

When directed, the balloons would be released in unison. There we stood, young and old and in-between…some "newbies" (that is what we called the new transplant patients) still with their masks on. As the countdown began to let go of the balloons,

I looked around at the fifty or so people surrounding me. Considering it was a 25 year anniversary, our group was relatively small. There were not many survivors in this battle and the few still standing deserved a Medal of Honor as much as the bravest of soldiers. When we all released the balloons, tears streamed down my cheeks as I watched them float away until they were only specks in the sky. It was such an emotional moment.

Shortly before we left the picnic, Maggie, the ward social worker, came over to chat. I had not seen her in several months because she had moved to another ward continuing her advocacy work for the patients. We hugged and after I sat down again she asked me if I had talked to Nancy lately. I told her that I had not heard from her in a long time and asked if she had any recent news from her. Reluctantly, Maggie told me that Nancy had died two days before the picnic. I looked up at the sky and shed more tears…she had deserved to be part of our illustrious group. Not a balloon was left in sight. We left with heavy hearts.

Chapter 19
July 1ˢᵗ to September 15ᵗʰ

We began our cycling training in mid-June in order to be in some semblance of shape for our vacation in September. For two weeks I felt as if there was no improvement in my conditioning. By the time I had cycled to our neighbor's mailbox which was only a mile down the road, I was bushed and could barely complete the remaining two miles. I wondered whether it was realistic to go on this vacation given the fact that there was no progress. One day I mentioned to Bob that I heard a noise on my bike while I was cycling and asked him to take it for a ride to analyze the problem. When he returned he had a silly grin and sheepishly told me that the brakes were sticking and the cables needed adjusting. After the repair, I hopped on for a test drive and nearly ended up in our mailbox at the speed with which I went down our driveway. I started laughing at the irony of it all! With the brakes fixed, I improved tremendously. By late August, I was cycling about 15-20 miles per outing…I knew I still had a long way to go, but I felt I would be able to hold my own on the vacation as long as there weren't too many taxing hills.

In July, I began to drive myself to the hospital for my monthly visits. Bob had been my chauffeur long enough and it was time for me to spread my wings and take charge of my appointments. Yes, I was still plagued by the fears, but as time went on I knew that my bone marrow was doing its job and the likelihood of my getting GVHD was doubtful. I was still careful, not to be would have been absurd. The doctors and nurses viewed me as the

"Poster Child" of the ward because I had exhibited none of the usual problems that went along with a bone marrow transplant and my excellent physical condition astounded them. The expressions on their faces when I announced that Bob and I were going to France on a cycling vacation were a combination of pride and worry. They knew there were still many risks for me, especially with going abroad, but they acknowledged that the psychological benefits outweighed the dangers. The goal was for all the bone marrow transplant patients to resume their normal lives or as close to what their lives had been as possible. They did suggest that I see a travel doctor who would guide me in terms of whether I needed any specific shots or what things I had to be careful of. I agreed wholeheartedly. Two weeks later, Bob and I saw the travel specialist and he asked us the details of our trip and what we would be doing. Since he already had my medical file from 3Z, he knew about my below normal immune system and was specifically concerned that I did not have my childhood immunizations. As a result of the transplant, I no longer had the benefit of the immunizations that I had received throughout childhood. Because my bone marrow had been destroyed, the new marrow was no different than that of an infant's, worse actually because with a baby the mother passed on her antibodies, and in my case there were none. Even though Pat had received his immunizations, he did not pass on this protection to me. I would need inoculations against such things as measles, mumps, rubella, and so on. Typically, the transplant protocol called for these immunizations to be administered approximately one year after transplant and I was still about seven weeks away from that. The reason for this one-year requirement was that these were "live" vaccines and if a patient had a compromised immune system, they might in fact come down with the very thing that they were being vaccinated against. Knowing I could not have these shots before my trip, he strongly suggested that I not be near any children or babies. That could prove lethal to me. He also had a list of foods I was not to eat, such as salads, fruit or anything raw that was washed in the local tap water. If I really wanted to eat a salad, he said, I could perhaps wash my own lettuce in bottled water. I laughed at that one…I could just see me in a hotel room with a bottle of Perrier washing lettuce, tomatoes, and cucumbers. I decided I could forego the salad and fruit but being a vegetarian, what would I be able to eat? I had already been advised by the hospital nutritionist that for the first year I could not eat any unpasteurized cheese or any moldy cheeses such as blue cheese and gorgonzola. That pained me because those types of cheeses were the ones I adored…I couldn't wait to be able to add them to my diet again. Thus, no salad, no fruit, no cheese... maybe I would just eat potato chips and drink wine for a week!!!!

The week before we left for France, I went to the hospital for another appointment. I was given several antibiotics in case I came down with a flu or cold that could lead to a lung infection and even a prescription if I got a bladder infection. All the bases were covered! Just before I left Kathy's office, Dr. Leber, another hematologist came in because he had heard I was going to France. He asked me if I spoke French, for what reason I did not understand, and I answered that yes I did. He said to me "Soyez prudent!" Translation…BE CAREFUL! I took that to heart. They all wished me a safe trip and Dr. Wasi asked that I send her a postcard from Paris. While in Paris, I found an "a propos" animated card of a butterfly sitting atop the Eiffel Tower which I mailed to her.

In mid-September, Bob, Owen and I, met at the airport and flew to Paris. I was terribly excited about this trip for many reasons but one was that I had never been to Paris and had always wanted to go. After a couple of days in Paris and doing such things as seeing the Louvre or walking along the Seine, we took the train to Dijon which was where we would be meeting our fellow cyclists as arranged by the tour operator. We took the opportunity to see a few sights in Dijon and for lunch we stopped at a sidewalk café that specialized in pizza. As I said before, pizza had always been my favorite food and thankfully, that was something that I was allowed to eat. I decided on a stone-fired pizza topped with Dijon mustard (yes), caramelized onions and various herbs. It was the best pizza I had ever eaten…for many reasons!

When the cyclists in our group met, we were bused to a beautiful chateau which would be the starting point of our cycling the following morning. I felt like a kid out of school even though I knew I had to be careful and I was. In the morning, we were outfitted with our bikes which had been matched to each cyclist by size, based on their height and weight. After a brief instruction of how the bikes worked regarding brakes, gears, etc., we were given our route notes (directions for the day's cycling). According to the directions, the first six kilometers would be completely uphill and Bob and I looked at each other deciding we would just do the best we could do. Yes, we had trained but this was a little bit above and beyond what our scope was. We all mounted our bikes and the experienced, keen cyclists sprinted past us and scooted up the hill. The first three switchbacks were manageable but then I began to tire and as I pedaled further and further, I kept hoping that the next one would be the summit of the hill. Bob was up ahead and turned around regularly to keep an eye on me and see how I was doing. I could hardly get enough air into my lungs and the muscles in my legs were screaming in pain but I persevered not wanting to give up. At one point, I started to weave back and forth across the road to give myself some relief from the constant uphill. At long last I could see the highest point and I was on the final switchback with the summit and the end of my struggle in sight.

Out of the blue, my eyes filled with tears and as I continued to pedal I began to cry like I had never cried before. With each tear that fell came the memories of the past 11 months – what I had been through and how unjust life had been – but then came the understanding that I had survived against all odds…I had survived because of a miracle. As I cycled alongside Bob, he looked over and was alarmed that I was crying "What's wrong?" he asked. I answered, "Nothing, I'm alive and I've made it!" We cycled side by side the remaining few feet to the peak of the hill and once on the other side, I threw caution to the wind and soared downhill in wild, joyful abandon. My new life had begun.

EPILOGUE

The last six years have been both wonderful and difficult. Bob and I retired three years ago and we have taken advantage of our freedom by travelling and taking part in what we love to do. I have remained GVHD-free, but I still carry the incessant fear associated with anything going wrong with my health. It is not that I worry about getting aplastic anemia again but moreover the worry of getting anything…even something as simple as a sinus infection. I wished I had sought counseling earlier rather than later.

Overall, our lives are richer. We appreciate the value of being healthy and will never take for granted that aspect of our lives. Bob and I know how very lucky I am to still be on this earth.

I have written my story based on my experience and how I perceived the information at the time. I felt that this was important because it dictated my state of mind during the transplant process. For full and complete protocols of a bone marrow transplant, the following links are excellent ones:
http://cumc.columbia.edu/dept/medicine/bonemarrow/bmtinfo.html
http://symptomchecker.about.com/od/child/legs/Diagnoses/bone-marrow-transplant.htm

BE HEALTHY, BE HAPPY!

WEBSITE RESOURCES TRANSPLANT SITES

List compiled by:
Kathleen Green, R.N. BScN, M.N., CON (C)
Acute Care Nurse Practitioner,
Allogeneic Bone Marrow Transplant Program,
J.C.C.H. Hamilton Health Sciences
and **Corinna McCracken**

Bone Marrow Transplant infonet
http://www.bmtinfonet.org
This is an American based site providing BMT patients and survivors a place they can turn to for accurate, easy-to-understand information. Their publications and web site are carefully reviewed by leading medical experts for accuracy.

Canadian Blood and Marrow Transplant Group
http://www.cbmtg.org/
CBMTG is a National, voluntary and multi-disciplinary organization providing leadership and promoting excellence in patient care, research and education in the field of blood and marrow transplantation.

Canadian Cancer Society
http://www.cancer.ca/
CCS is a national, community-based organization of volunteers whose mission is the eradication of cancer and the enhancement of the quality of life of people living with cancer. It provides many educational resources and community resources including transportation assistance.

Cancer.Net
http://www.cancer.net/portal/site/patient
It brings the expertise and resources of the American Society of Clinical Oncology (ASCO), the voice of the world's cancer physicians, to people living with cancer and those who care for and care about them. ASCO is composed of more than 28,000 oncologists globally who are the leaders in advancing cancer care. All the information and content on Cancer.Net was developed and approved by the cancer doctors who are members of ASCO, making Cancer.Net the most up-to-date and trusted resource for cancer information on the Internet.

Centre for Internation Blood and Marrow Transplant Research
http://www.cibmtr.org/
CIBMTR collaborates with the global scientific community to advance hematopoietic cell transplantation and cellular therapy research worldwide. A combined research program of the National Marrow Donor Program® and the Medical College of Wisconsin, CIBMTR facilitates critical research that has led to increased survival and an enriched quality of life for thousands of patients. Its prospective and observational research is accomplished through scientific and statistical expertise, a large network of transplant centers and a clinical database of more than 300,000 transplant recipients.

Foundation for the Accreditation of Cellular Therapy
   http://www.factwebsite.org/
FACT establishes standards for high quality medical and laboratory practice in cellular therapies. The main objective of FACT is to promote high quality patient care and laboratory performance in the belief that a valid accreditation must assess both clinical and laboratory aspects.

The Leukemia & Lymphoma Society
   http://www.leukemia-lymphoma.org/hm_lls
LLS is the world's largest voluntary health organization dedicated to funding blood cancer research, education and patient services. LLS's mission: Cure leukemia, lymphoma, Hodgkin's disease and myeloma, and improve the quality of life of patients and their families.

National Bone Marrow Transplant Link
   http://www.nbmtlink.org/
The mission of this organization is to help patients, caregivers, and families cope with the social and emotional challenges of bone marrow/stem cell transplant from diagnosis through survivorship by providing vital information and personalized support services. Available to order: "Caregivers' Guide For Bone Marrow/Stem Cell Transplant"

National Institutes of Health (NIH)
   http://www.cancer.gov/
This site is a part of the U.S. Department of Health and Human Services, the nation's medical research agency—making important medical discoveries that improve health and save lives.

National Marrow Donor Program
   http://www.marrow.org/
An American website that helps to find matches in the U.S. and helps to advance medical research. This site also offers information to patients and families about the bone marrow transplant.

OncoLink
   http://www.oncolink.org/
Provides comprehensive information about specific types of cancer, updates on cancer treatments and news about research advances. The information is updated everyday and provided at various levels, from introductory to in-depth. If you are interested in learning about cancer, you will benefit from visiting OncoLink.

OneMatch Stem Cell and Marrow Network
   http://onematch.ca/
It's mission is to secure, in an expeditious way, donors for Canadian bone marrow transplant patients and for patients abroad.

ACKNOWLEDGEMENTS

There are many people to thank in the writing of this book. Foremost, I thank my husband, Bob, for always being there for me. To my brother Pat; your support was as important to me as "The Golden Juice." Thank you both for saving my life! Also, thank you to Mom, Linda and our wonderful family and friends who were so supportive during my illness.

Bringing this book to fruition was not an easy task both from a writing standpoint and the re-living of all the memories. Were it not for Bob's and everyone's encouragement; my story may never have seen the light of day.

I would also like to thank Laura Masterson for designing the book cover as well as the chapter graphics. My sincerest gratitude to all who contributed in the editing process.

Made in the USA
Middletown, DE
15 January 2018